Voices Against Trafficking™

ENDORSEMENTS

"*Voices Against Trafficking: Courage is Contagious* is a powerful testament to the courage and compassion of everyday people who chose to act when others might have looked away. In a world often overwhelmed by indifference, this gripping collection of real-life stories reminds us that one voice—one person—can spark meaningful change. Each account is a rallying cry against injustice and a beacon of hope for those still in the shadows.

More than just a book, *Voices Against Trafficking: Courage is Contagious*, is a movement—one that empowers readers to believe in their ability to make a difference. Whether you're an advocate, a survivor, or someone searching for purpose, these stories will move you, challenge you, and leave you inspired to take action."

—**Chris Meek**, Ed.D., Host of Next Steps Forward

"From the very beginning, *Voices Against Trafficking: Courage is Contagious* captivated my attention. This powerful collection of true personal stories is a stark reminder that human trafficking is happening all around us—often hiding in plain sight. Traffickers continue their crimes largely because so many of us don't know what to look for. That's why it's critical for each of us to learn the warning signs and understand how and where to report suspicious activity. *Voices Against Trafficking* ignites a sense of urgency and inspires readers to take impactful action, and help bring an end to this crisis."

—**Michael Gier**, Award-Winning Filmmaker

"*Voices Against Trafficking*™ – *Courage is Contagious* is a powerful and vital collection that amplifies the unwavering voices of those fighting against the horrific crime of human trafficking. It's a testament to the strength of unity and a crucial call to action for individuals and nations alike. *Voices Against Trafficking* is essential reading for anyone seeking to understand and combat modern slavery."

—**Michael Botte**, Michael Botte Band

"The scourge of human trafficking continues to be a plague throughout the world. We cannot afford to be blind or silent to the reality of this despicable crime. *Voices of Human Trafficking* is an organization that is on the front lines in combating this evil that enslaves children and adults into sex trafficking. Their new book takes you on a gripping journey that shines a light on this sinister trade that operates in the shadows of society. Furthermore, I pray *Voices Against Trafficking* will help you raise your Voices Against Human Trafficking."

—**Kelly Wright**, Journalist

"We are deeply honored to endorse *Voices Against Trafficking*™– *Courage is Contagious: Uniting Voices and Nations in the War Against Human Slavery*. This powerful work shines a light on one of the darkest issues of our time—human trafficking and sexual exploitation—while also offering hope, action, and a pathway for individuals and communities to be part of the solution.

Voices Against Trafficking not only informs but also inspires. The stories, insights, and calls to action are a testament to the courage of survivors, advocates, and allies around the world who are fighting for justice and dignity. Courage is Contagious is more than just a title—it's a truth that runs through every page of this important publication.

We wholeheartedly support the mission of Voices Against Trafficking and believe *Voices Against Trafficking* will be a powerful tool in awakening hearts and mobilizing efforts worldwide to end modern-day slavery. We encourage everyone to read it, share it, and become part of this vital movement."

With respect and solidarity,

—**Maureen and Herbert Dembe**, More Hope Ministry (Uganda)

"I'll never forget the day the county Sheriff's Deputy told me we had a human trafficking recruiter in our student body. As a high school administrator, I was shocked! This student had been groomed to the extent she was now recruiting young teenagers to enter the same nightmare life she had begun only a few years ago. Please take to heart that human trafficking is a real threat to everyone, even, or perhaps especially, where you don't expect it. Thank you *Voices Against Trafficking* for getting the news out about this travesty and providing hope for those caught in its snare!"

—**Dr. Alice A. Dewittie**, Ed.D

"In a world where it's easy to feel powerless against overwhelming social issues, *Voices Against Trafficking*™ – *Courage is Contagious* delivers a potent reminder that individual action matters. This compelling collection of firsthand accounts showcases ordinary people who, upon witnessing troubling situations, chose courage over complacency. The contributors—including the fearless Andi Buerger who shares her own journey of escape—demonstrate how recognizing warning signs and taking decisive action can transform or even save lives. Their stories dismantle the common excuse that one person can't make a difference, instead offering both inspiration and practical guidance for readers who might encounter similar situations. More than just a book for human rights activists, this collection serves as an essential blueprint for anyone who has ever witnessed injustice and wondered, "What can I possibly do?"

—**Dennis J. Pitocco**, Founder & Chief Reimaginator, 360° Nation

"Veteran Activist Andi Buerger compiles a compelling narrative that ignites the inner flame of all those who understand the devastating history of human trafficking, while enlightening others to the heroism of everyday people battling an extraordinary evil. *Voices Against Trafficking: Courage is Contagious* is a must read and share many times over."

—**Lisa Noel Babbage**, PhD., Founder of Maranatha House Ministries

"Andi Buerger has done it again. She blends the truth of child trafficking with riveting stories of experts who see the nuances of a culture that has normalized exposure to adult sexual content. This is a must read for anybody who wants to protect children (as well as adults in a noisy culture) that has forgotten what protection means.

We all say that we care for children but what does that mean? If it doesn't include action to protect innocence, it's not a priority. Today, porn is the wallpaper for children exposed to adult sexual content. Read this book and decide what you are called to do."

—**Mary Bawden**, Founder, Dance Awareness: No Child Exploited

"My wife and I have been honored to support Andi Buerger's work against human trafficking for over a decade now. We have watched this non-profit grow from its infancy to a full fledged group that carries a much needed word for those who can't speak on their own. This group has grown and captured momentum as more and more families and organizations have rallied to this cause. Everyone who hears Andi's story and the stories of those whom she champions are moved and empowered to join in VAT's endeavors."

—**Pastor Mike Ferry,** Transformation Ministries

"Human trafficking is a worldwide epidemic, more than a $150 billion industry, where human rights are non-existent. Andi Buerger and contributors give us a glimpse into the world of this inhumane industry of human slavery in *Voices Against Trafficking*™—*Courage is Contagious*. It's happening all around us, and most people are unaware of the signs that something nefarious may be unfolding right in front of them. Once you read this book, your eyes will be opened. It's been said that Courage is Fear that's said its prayers. Be Courageous. You can make a difference."

—**Teresa Velardi**, Publisher and Host of Conversations That Make A Difference

"I've had the privilege to receive a copy of *Voices Against Trafficking: Courage Is Contagious* by Andi Buerger. It's encouraging to know there are advocates. Together, we can reach millions of people, both to inform and to help survivors heal.

Reading Voices Against Trafficking brings the issues to light and has inspired me to talk more openly about my own experiences. Today I have more compassion and more inspiration. I recommend *Voices Against Trafficking: Courage Is Contagious* for every survivor. Every church should have a copy. This book will inspire and uplift the troubled spirit. It's true that the journey to healing is challenging, but resources like this can empower individuals to break free from their past and seek support. Voices of encouragement to others facing similar struggles is vital—reminding them that they are not alone, and that their stories matter, can inspire many to find their own paths to freedom and healing."

—**Cindy H. Nene**, Admin. Director, West Coast high school administrator I was shocked Shipping-WCS, Cote d'Ivoire (Africa)

"As a survivor, global advocate, Consecrated Bishop in the Lord's Church, and Executive Director of Woman At The Well Transition Center, I am blessed to endorse *Voices Against Trafficking*™—*Courage is Contagious: Uniting Voices and Nations in the War Against Human Slavery*. Rooted in faith and driven by a divine calling to bring freedom to the captives, this work is a testament to God's relentless love for the oppressed.

Through inspiring testimonies and Spirit-led insights, Courage is Contagious not only exposes the darkness of human trafficking but also proclaims the hope of redemption found in Christ. Each story echoes Psalm 34:18—"The Lord is close to the brokenhearted"—reminding us that no soul is too lost for His grace.

Voices Against Trafficking is more than information; it is a prayer in action. It stirs our hearts to intercede, equips our hands to serve, and challenges our feet to march in the footsteps of Jesus, who proclaimed freedom for the captives (Luke 4:18). We stand in agreement with *Voices Against Trafficking's* mission and pray that every reader will be emboldened by faith, empowered by truth, and moved to join this crusade against modern-day slavery."

—**Bishop Donna L. Hubbard**, Survivor Leader/Executive Director, Woman At The Well Transition Center

VOICES AGAINST TRAFFICKING™

COURAGE IS CONTAGIOUS:
UNITING VOICES AND NATIONS IN THE WAR AGAINST HUMAN SLAVERY

ANDI BUERGER, JD

NEW YORK
LONDON • NASHVILLE • MELBOURNE • VANCOUVER

VOICES AGAINST TRAFFICKING

Courage is Contagious: Uniting Voices and Nations in the War Against Human Slavery

© 2025 Andi Buerger

All rights reserved. No portion of this book may be reproduced, stored in a retrieval system, or transmitted in any form or by any means—electronic, mechanical, photocopy, recording, scanning, or other—except for brief quotations in critical reviews or articles, without the prior written permission of the publisher.

Scripture quotations taken from The Holy Bible, New International Version® NIV® Copyright © 1973, 1978, 1984, 2011 by Biblica, Inc.™ Used by permission. All rights reserved worldwide.

Published in New York, New York, by Morgan James Publishing. Morgan James is a trademark of Morgan James, LLC. www.MorganJamesPublishing.com

Proudly distributed by Publishers Group West®

A **FREE** ebook edition is available for you or a friend with the purchase of this print book.

CLEARLY SIGN YOUR NAME ABOVE

Instructions to claim your free ebook edition:
1. Visit MorganJamesBOGO.com
2. Sign your name CLEARLY in the space above
3. Complete the form and submit a photo of this entire page
4. You or your friend can download the ebook to your preferred device

ISBN 9781636986234 paperback
ISBN 9781636986241 ebook
Library of Congress Control Number: 2025931059

Cover Design by:
Ale Urquide

Interior Design by:
Chris Treccani
www.3dogcreative.net

Morgan James is a proud partner of Habitat for Humanity Peninsula and Greater Williamsburg. Partners in building since 2006.

Get involved today! Visit: www.morgan-james-publishing.com/giving-back

DEDICATION

*"Go and get the cast out, the downtrodden, the least likely, those that others have given up on …
and tell them I have chosen them to be My jewels.
I will dig them out of the pits of life, chisel them according to My will, polish them up, and set them aside as My peculiar treasure."*
-Unknown

ACKNOWLEDGEMENTS

It is the cast out and the forgotten, the invisible innocents whose lives have been shattered and stolen for profit, their shadowed remains left to perish—much like the man The Good Samaritan found alongside the dusty road in biblical times–to whom this book is dedicated. The wounded stranger in the parable had been passed up by others until *one* came along and sacrificed his time, money, and resources so the stranger could live.

It is for these "peculiar treasures" that God has called this book into existence. It is for those who have been so deeply wounded, so desperately emptied of innocence and even life, that this book is dedicated. There are many sitting on the side of life's road if we would only take the time to look and to act without reservation, without fear of judgment by onlookers and those who refuse to offer compassion or aid.

There have been many hands involved with the compilation of this book. To them, I offer my deepest gratitude for their sacrifice. Specifically, my dear friend and first "comrade in arms" for Voices Against Trafficking™, Hon. Blanquita "BQ" Cullum. She not only saw the vision God inspired in me, but grasped the greater picture for generations yet to be. She has worked tirelessly to bring others of influence and means to the fight for our children, for all innocents, and for every child of God.

Without the literal presence of the "magnificent seven" members of Congress who *originally* heralded the need for more voices to engage in the fight against human trafficking, the impact Voices Against Trafficking™ is making would not be as deep and certainly not worldwide. They are Representative (Ret.) Pete Olson (TX-22), Representative Jim Costa (CA-16), Representative Debbie Lesko (AZ-08), Representative Ann Wagner (MO-02), Representative Chip Roy (TX-21), Representative Chris Smith (NJ-04), and Representative (Ret.). Greg Walden (OR-02).

The work of every Charter Member and Charter Media Member of Voices Against Trafficking™ is essential to the future of all children and innocents. I cannot be more grateful for their sacrifices to help reach the voiceless through our 501c3 nonprofit organization.

Of course, kudos to the ever-patient artisans who crafted the book design, inside and out, and who edited many, many words: Morgan James Publishing, Morgan Visser, Amanda Reill.

As important as those names above, and the many more not listed, are my husband, Ed, and our daughter, Leah Jane.

In my life, I am *called* to be a treasure hunter. I learned that from God, my heavenly Father, through the sacrifice of His Son, Jesus Christ. It was God who pulled me out of the pit of evil so I could shine brightly enough to find other peculiar treasures for the glory of His heavenly kingdom.

- Andi

CONTENTS

Acknowledgements . . . . *xv*
Introduction . . . . *xxiii*

1
Behind the Curtain
By Lisa Babbage, Ph.D

11
Filmmaking and Faith – Partnering to End Human Trafficking
By Andi Buerger, JD

21
Uganda: Prevention and Response to Trafficking in Persons
By Detective Nusura Kemigisha

25
Wholesome to Hypersexualized: What Happened to Children's Dance?
By Mary Margaret Bawden

37

Actress Anne Heche – Crazy?
A Survivor Speaks Out
By Andi Buerger, JD

41

Protecting Everyday People from Everyday Threats
By Hunter Allen

43

Border Security: Chaos Kills
By Rodney Scott

49

Overcoming Exploitation: An Overview of
Expressive Arts in Restorative Care
By Danielle Freitag, LADC

61

Turning a Million Eyes to Save Lives
By Deborah S. Sigmund

67

Courage Is Contagious: The True Story of
Crystal Chen's Fight for Human Rights
By Andi Buerger, JD

77

The Ripples
By Jeff Wagner

81
The "Wicked Good" Investigation
*By Eric Caron, U.S. Special Agent
& U.S. Diplomat (Ret.)*

113
PTSD: How To Face The
Unseen Monster and Live Forward
By Andi Buerger, JD

121
To Model or Not To Model? Know The Risks
By Pamela Privette

125
Healing Requires Safety
By K. L. Byles

131
Combating Human Trafficking:
Tackling Demand with Federal Accountability
By Chris Meek, Ed.D

135
Lack of Financial and Human Resources Fuels
Human Trafficking, Sexual Exploitation,
and Illegal Immigration Worldwide
By Randy Purham

145
Building Bridges: Turning What
Was Meant for Evil Into Good
By Casandra Diamond and Mikhaela Gray-Beerman

159
How Ninety Seconds Changed My Life:
The Line Between Success and Defeat
By Andi Buerger, JD

Helplines and Hotlines. 165
About the Author 169

"It's not about right versus left.
It's about right versus **wrong**."

HON. BLANQUITA CULLUM

INTRODUCTION

More voices.

Over and over, those words echoed in my mind. Words that would wake me up in the middle of the night until I could no longer sleep. I wrestled with that echo of a familiar voice I remembered from my early childhood. The one that saved my life on more than one occasion. It was what I call a "God nudge"—a prompting that it was time for *more*. A nudge to inspire action that I might not otherwise choose to take.

This time, however, God not only nudged me, but He also nudged my great friend, Blanquita "BQ" Cullum. A genuine force for the voiceless and a brilliant media strategist, BQ partnered with me in what has now become the greatest human rights movement to date: ending twenty-first-century slavery, also known as human trafficking. *Human* trafficking. Not drugs. Not guns. Living, breathing innocent babies, children, teens, and young adults.

Human trafficking, in its simplest definition, is the buying and selling of human beings for profit and/or perversion. Familial trafficking is the same activity conducted by family members, often resulting in generational trafficking with untold numbers of victims. Familial predators use their bloodline relationship with their readily accessible prey as a cloak of protection, making it harder to identify and prosecute accordingly. In that respect, victimized children are trapped; they are slaves to the family members perpetrating horrific acts against their own bloodline.

The fight to end human trafficking is no small task. I knew that when my husband, Ed, and I established Beulah's Place, a 501(c)3 nonprofit organization, in 2008. Beulah's Place provided temporary shelter services to at-risk homeless teen boys and girls in danger of sex trafficking, severe abuse, neglect, and other criminally predatory activities for fourteen years. Our organization assisted more than three hundred teens who needed to complete their high school education, acquire and maintain viable employment, learn independent living skills, and successfully transition back into their communities with little to no assistance. Many received scholarships to college, earned degrees, made the Dean's List, and even continued on to postgraduate studies.

In September 2020, Donald W. Washington, Director of the U.S. Marshals Service, was interviewed following yet another successful rescue of missing children, this time in northeastern Ohio. He said, "Every forty seconds, a child is abducted in the United States." *Every forty seconds.* Every community here and abroad has predators looking for easy prey. Whether a child is eight or eighteen years old, he or she is at risk simply because many communities still refuse to believe that human trafficking happens "here" – in their neighborhood, their schools, their churches. In Central Oregon, we have had leaders in our community as well as at the state level who refused to acknowledge human trafficking as a real issue. Unfortunately, there are victims who would disagree and will not receive the rehabilitation and resources for recovery that they deserve – providing they feel safe enough to even come forward and report their experiences.

Despite the great successes of Beulah's Place, I felt there was more that could be done. While my voice was powerful, persuasive, and passionate, it was still just one voice. I needed more. *More voices.*

The God nudge was now becoming noticeably persistent. For decades, I have shared my personal story as a survivor of child sex trafficking, unspeakable abuse and torture, and times of imprisonment by immediate and extended family members. From six months to seventeen years old, my birth mother was the primary orchestrator of all familial evil. The last time she tried to take my life, I was seventeen. Back in the 1960s, there simply wasn't a place or a way for a trapped child to get help, especially when family members were involved. Those predators were covered by the bloodline, and they knew it. No scream or desperate plea would ever be heard, let alone reported.

I speak because it is the truth of my journey that helps to open ears, hearts, and, yes, in some cases, personal pocketbooks to help bring healing and hope to the innocent children I help rescue. The youth at Beulah's Place ran to the streets because the streets seemed safer than what they were running from at home. My story also shares the hope that both victims and their communities can be successful together in fighting against the evil of human trafficking.

My voice speaks for the voiceless who desperately hope that someone, somehow, will find them, bring them back to safety, help them heal, and catch the violators who have stolen their innocence and liberties as human beings. These young people hope that their predator(s) will be fully prosecuted, locked up for life, or die. No parole. No early release. Straight-up confinement until death. Those are the only two ways a victim can ever truly feel relief or feel safe from the criminal sadist(s) who ripped their innocence and their life into millions of pieces. Some of those pieces may heal over time with qualified therapy and support systems, but most do not. It is a life sentence for the one victimized, which is why self-medication, chronic pain and illness, excessive coping mechanisms, and self-destructive behavior demons show up. *I know.*

I am grateful my child's heart was open the day God spoke to it when I was five years old. My birth mother had already told me that she could "take me out" any day she wanted. I thought if I was dead, then at least I would be at peace. I would never have to go in that house again and be used beyond words for pervasive acts. Since she was capable of killing me, why not just end my life myself and beat her to the punch?

I sat on the curb in front of my house, waiting for a car to come by fast enough to kill me when I jumped in front of it. While I was waiting, I looked up into the huge blue sky. I wondered how far it reached. Who made it? Was there someone bigger than the people who hurt me? Then I thought, why aren't there any cars coming down my street today?

This is not the plan I have for you. Suicide is not the answer.

I listened intently to the quiet voice within my heart that seemed to know why I was on the curb. *This is not the plan I have for you.* Again, I pondered that voice. More importantly, I believed that voice with the only words of hope I had heard in my five years of life. I went up the driveway and stood against the garage door, still thinking about the voice in my heart. Before I knew it, these words came out of my mouth as if an answer to what I had heard: *If you keep me alive, I will do whatever you call me to do.*

God's voice. It was the nudge I needed to keep moving forward despite the great pain, agony, and indescribable heartache that led me to two more suicide attempts. Again, in those instances, God showed up. Just as He had when I was five years old. It was a good thing, too, because it took my birth mother ninety-one years to pass from this life. She was never caught, prosecuted, or reported. In those early days, most people didn't even talk about child abuse, let alone "organized" child abuse for perversion's sake, in my case. If she had been able to make a profit off of me or her son, I'm not sure I would still be here to share my voice.

The death of a predator is a particular relief for any victim. No longer can that person ever physically enter my life, threaten my happiness, destroy my security, or inflict evil on another person in any possible way, especially a child. No matter how much therapy, prayer, and healing a victim receives, there is always an underlying awareness that a predator's face will again show up in their life.

My voice as a survivor-leader who has made choices each and every day – not without mistakes–counts for a lot in some circles. Proof that victims with a background similar to mine, whether to a greater or lesser degree, can be successful in relationships and succeed in finding a "new normal" is critical for those who feel they walk this path of pain alone. One voice is a good start, but it would count for more if others from all facets of human trafficking – prevention, education, awareness, rescue and rehabilitation of victims across borders, and legislative accountability – could come together as a collective and collaborative voice against trafficking.

Inspiration hit me quickly one night in the wee hours of the morning. I heard that same gentle voice I have heard throughout my life speak three simple words: *Voices Against Trafficking*™. I waited for the clock to move forward enough to call BQ in

Washington, D.C., so I could share the revelation. She agreed it was a truly God-inspired name, perfectly suited to cover a powerful global movement. We began to create an entity that would bring all people and organizations into one "hub" while maintaining their individual or organizational identities.

Independent agencies, nonprofit organizations, corporations, social service groups, houses of worship, national and international legislators, human rights leaders, and everyday individuals – all speaking as *one* voice. From a retail clerk to members of Congress, teachers to auto mechanics, college students to health practitioners, single parents to retired military members – *every* voice will count. *Every* voice can be part of the solution in our collective fight to turn the tide on the depraved predators who are allowed to run rampant in the U.S. and around the globe.

In 2019, more than twenty organizations from the U.S. and Mexico gathered on Capitol Hill in Washington, D.C., to speak out for all victims of human trafficking. Over 200 attendees, including media members from the U.S. and Mexico, non-partisan members of Congress such as Rep. Pete Olson, TX (Ret.), Rep. Jim Costa, CA, Rep. Greg Walden, OR (Ret.), Rep. Ann Wagner, MO, Rep. Debbie Lesko, AZ, and Rep. Chip Roy, TX, and members of the general public met to bring greater understanding and awareness of the human trafficking crisis.

While the nature of depravity may never be obliterated, the number of innocents who are unwillingly coerced into the more than $160 billion transnational criminal enterprise that benefits predators (and those who cover up for predators) can be greatly reduced. More than two-thirds of that $160 billion revenue comes from sex trafficking. Demand drives profits.

Without demand, there is no profit. Without profit, there is no point in doing business.

Without intercession by millions of voices speaking as *one*, human trafficking in the United States will overtake drug trafficking as the number one illegal enterprise in a year or two, if not sooner. I have often said, *"When we allow our children to be sold, to be used as a commodity, to be violated, persecuted, neglected, discarded, and preyed upon by criminal influences, we deteriorate as a civilized community. There is **nothing civilized** about exploiting the weak, the innocent, and the vulnerable for profit."*

We need *more voices* against human trafficking, especially the sex trafficking of children.

We need *more voices* against cartels selling children at the border.

We need *more voices* internationally who agree to prosecute anyone transporting victims across borders.

We need *more voices* who are less concerned with political or social stature and more concerned with being on the side of human rights for every human being in the U.S., Mexico, and the other 193 countries worldwide.

Never has there been a more urgent time for us to bring our best game as global citizens against human trafficking. Twenty-first-century slavery is a *crime* against history. It is a *crime* against humanity. More than ever, your voice is essential to our success.

Six decades into my life, I am beyond amazed at how far a child from nowhere, with nothing to her name, and who felt like yesterday's garbage for the first thirty years of her life can go simply by using her voice. The voice God inspired in me so many years ago has been leading me forward despite tremendous adversities physically, financially, and emotionally as I work to rescue those with backgrounds similar to mine.

I am greatly blessed with an extraordinary husband and a beautifully brilliant adult daughter, who we officially adopted in 2020. I have friends who support me, hundreds of kids who can "live forward" because of the intercession they received, chairmanship of Voices Against Trafficking™, a successful magazine called *Voices Of Courage*, a music album called Broken Treasures – The Inspiration Album, and so much more. These are some of the things that make the difficult days – when PTSD or daily pain deter my energies – more manageable. If even for my daughter, for just one of the hundreds of victims served by my efforts, the life I endured was worth it.

As long as there are victims, Voices Against Trafficking™ will continue its quest for every human's rights to be protected, not just those of the predators on every social level who have no fear of prosecution or definitive punishment in almost any town, city, state, and country around the globe. Our combined voices will continue to create momentum and leverage to forge deeper and more impacting paths in the war against human trafficking. Together, tens of thousands can be saved and their persecutors brought to justice.

Every human being deserves to live freely and safely. Human rights are a human issue. There are no politics or agendas for the victims who remain enslaved by vicious criminals. I invite you to join Voices Against Trafficking™.

More voices.

Be that voice today. If not now, when?

Andi Buerger, JD Her *Voices Of Courage*™ magazine is available online at VoicesOfCourage.media with a television program, also titled *Voices Of Courage*™, due out in 2026. Andi's work continues to appear in numerous publications, books, online news outlets, and bestselling titles including *Everyday Triumph - Extraordinary Stories of Hope, Resilience, and Impact,* by Chris Meek, Ed.D.

BEHIND THE CURTAIN
By Lisa Babbage, Ph.D

I *will never forget his hands – the way he held her.* These words have echoed in my mind ever since I came face-to-face with human trafficking.

The more we travel, the more we are in the presence of traffickers: people whose business it is to trade or make illegal business dealings with women, girls, boys, and even young men who are forced into modern-day slavery. In many countries, especially throughout Europe and the rest of the West, human trafficking takes place right under our noses – on railways, interstate buses, at stadium events, in shopping malls, and in airports. And yes, it is happening in plain sight. Witnessing it momentarily takes us behind the curtain of an intricate web of evil plaguing every continent and community.

I first saw this perpetrator on a layover in Charlotte, North Carolina. My background in the anti-trafficking movement caused him to stand out like a flashing red light in my line of sight. The littlest clues, like the way he held the infant in his hands, gave his motive away. There was no doubt in my mind that I was witnessing an interstate trafficking operation unfold.

She couldn't have been more than six months old. Not walking yet, but old enough to sit up with assistance. She was dressed like a Christmas present, which is perhaps what bothered me the most. It was September and I was ending what had been a long business trip bound for Georgia.

There were only a few precious minutes between my flights. Times when I might typically visit the vendors and pick up something for my grandson. Or better yet, stretch my legs by walking down to the end of the terminal and back. Today was different. I had left my phone on the plane and had been waiting for the other passengers to disembark so a crew member could retrieve it. Even though my departure terminal was just around the corner, I was frazzled. Not only would I miss my long-awaited stroll past shops filled with things I didn't need, but I might miss my flight altogether if I stood here much longer. As it was, I didn't really have a choice. I wasn't going home without my phone.

Business travelers understand this frantic feeling perhaps more than anyone else. So desperate to get home after a long and weary journey, you just want to put your AirPods in, tuck your head down, and chill on the last leg of your trip. This is what I was hoping for. But when I rounded the corner to my terminal, my eye instantly found this infant. Like any grandmother, I made note of her.

She was fussy, perhaps typical for her age in that way. The man carrying her fumbled her from one shoulder to another then sat her on a counter surrounded by people, many of whom were women. I found myself staring as he attempted to handle her; the pacifier in her mouth did not do the trick of soothing this baby. The longer I stared, the more I became convinced that this man did not know this child very well.

The way he never made eye contact with her, the way he attempted to hold her with one hand as he played on his phone with the other, the way she responded to his touch were all consistent with the way a fledgling sitter might interact after meeting a child for the first time. There was no closeness, even though they were physically close. There was no emotion on his face. Nothing that would indicate the two travelers were family. Absolutely nothing.

He was dressed casually, almost too comfortable. His pants hung low on his hips and his t-shirt was stained. He had no luggage and didn't appear to be carrying a wallet. His hoodie was misshapen and a bit too small to actually zip up. His hair was disheveled, and there were signs of a patchy five-o'clock shadow forming on his face. He was a mess. She, on the other hand, was impeccably dressed. Even with her tear-stained face, she looked as precious as a doll. Her red and white Christmas-y dress made her look like a present, all done up with bows. She was wearing white tights. I'll never forget how cute her feet looked even as he rotated her from hip to hip, trying to keep her silent.

Perhaps the stain on his shirt was from the baby, I pondered, trying to pull myself back from where my mind had already gone. Perhaps she was dressed up to see her mother? Was this father trying to show his wife that he could handle being alone with the baby? These were the ways I tried to make myself ignore the discomfort I felt in the pit of my stomach as I watched this man with the child. I had to do something to break my stare; my fixation would eventually be noticeable to others.

Today's air travel is not what it used to be. Even though mask restrictions had been lifted, people were avoiding each other. People had become distant over the past two years, and it showed. I just wanted to get home without incident, yet here

I found myself in the middle of an unfolding story I was sure I didn't want to read. That's when I forced myself to look away from this man who was only a few feet from me on the other side of the counter.

My eyes found another person to notice. It was a woman standing mere inches from the man and the baby, staring at him as I had just been. She looked up, and we locked eyes. I knew then the observations I had been mulling over in my mind were not mine alone. She saw the same thing I saw, and I knew I had to do something. But what? They were already calling the military and first-class passengers to board this flight we had all been waiting for.

I ran around the corner to my previous gate and found the attendant who retrieved my phone. Although I was trying to be inconspicuous, I'm sure I was a bit frantic by the time I got the words out: "Where is security?"

The agent gave me a puzzled look. There was no noise in the terminal, except for the boarding announcements and elderly golf cart transport that hummed in the background. Everyone was ready to go home, and it was obvious to me that this attendant didn't understand my sense of urgency because he failed to answer.

So I repeated my question, "Where is TSA security?"

"You have to go back through security to find a TSA agent." Go back through security? I would surely miss my flight, the last one of the night. There was no way that was going to happen.

"Isn't there a security phone or supervisor I can speak to?" All I could think about were the options I had at my disposal. If this man was truly trafficking an infant, what proof did I have? I doubted anyone would take my hunch seriously, and I didn't want to be dismissed as hysterical. Perhaps this was a travel companion in an adoption situation. Maybe he was simply transporting her for a legitimate business reason. But all of these seemingly plausible excuses for his demeanor with the child just didn't hold water.

As a veteran teacher, I had seen countless dads with their children. This was not how they acted. Even the expectant couples I counseled at my local pregnancy center were more in tune with their unborn child than this man was with the one in his arms. She was still fussing. Her voice, muffled by his shoulder, occasionally broke through. I ran to a gate which was on the other side of the airport where my flight was boarding, hoping to find the supervisor I had been directed to. The woman I had locked eyes with had moved to the other side of the terminal. She had apparently won the battle with her mind and successfully stifled the warning signs she witnessed.

Calmly, I approached the two gate agents standing there and asked for the supervisor by name. When she identified herself, I asked, "Do you have to show identification to bring a child under twelve on a plane?" This seemed logical enough and would end this riddle in my head. I remembered taking my daughter on a trip to Australia when she was two. The airline wanted everything but a blood sample to prove her age and our relationship. Surely, not much had changed, I thought. But sadly, this was not the case. The supervisor proceeded to tell me that for the past several years, TSA has not required identification for minors. It is up to the airline to decide whether or not to ask for ID for minors traveling with adults.[1] Even if *this* man's intentions were honorable, what about all the others?

---

1   Jenni Wilitz, "Minor Child Identification & Airline Travel," *USA Today*, last modified November 28, 2017, https://traveltips.usatoday.com/minor-child-identification-airline-travel-52409.html.

Suddenly, I realized how big this loophole could be. Many of us consider human trafficking as this blight that only occurs in dark alleys late at night, with prostitutes, drug addicts, and runaways. But having been connected with two anti-trafficking organizations for nearly a decade, I had come to know the ugly truth about sex, labor, and organ trafficking. It is happening all over the world, in broad daylight, with people you would not expect to be caught up in this global burden. Could this infant be another victim?

As I walked away from the gate supervisor, I decided to call some of my partners in the anti-trafficking space. Two answered and directed me to the National Human Trafficking Hotline, the number I was looking for. It had been saved in my phone, but at that moment, I could not locate it. After opening a complaint with the hotline, I returned to the scene of the potential crime. He was making her a bottle.

This was the second bottle he had attempted to give her in the 20-minute span of time since I first laid eyes on this child. I remember distinctly because he never burped her from the first bottle. All of the memories of my children at this age came flooding back. She will surely spit up if he does not burp her. He is using the bottle to silence her. Why isn't he rocking her instead? Why is she so dressed up for travel? No one would put a baby in a fancy dress and then get on a red-eye. The two just did not go together.

I began taking photos of this man. I wanted a record for the hotline, just in case. He was so preoccupied with his phone that he never noticed me. I tried to remember details about him so I could report my concerns to the Atlanta police department when I landed. We were on the same flight; perhaps something could be done while we were in the air. He stood up, thankfully, so I could gauge his height and weight. That's when the whole package literally came into view for me.

He was not wearing a wedding ring. What new mother would send her six-month-old baby on a plane with a dad who didn't have the "dad gene" yet? Her diaper bag still had the tags on, as if it were just purchased today. He was dressed like an undercover security guard while she was dressed for a fashion show. He did not board with all the other parents who gladly took advantage of the pre-boarding option to get their children settled. Instead, he waited his turn, like everyone else who was seated in the rear of the plane.

When she finally did burp, he looked surprised, actually making eye contact with her for the first time. She was miserable, and he was captured by whatever was on his phone. His large frame and bone structure dwarfed her petite physique. While she was young, it was obvious that she was either a preemie or had a very different bone structure to the man who was holding her. In spite of everything I could try to reason away, I had always been naturally good at guessing people's ethnic heritage. These two travelers were of different ethnicities, even though they were both Caucasian. It was like night and day.

Indeed, even if he was selling this child to an infertile couple who would love and care for her, what I was watching should be a serious concern for any parent.

I decided to be the last person to board for two reasons: I wanted to make sure he actually boarded our flight, and secondly, I wanted to see if there was an Airline Ambassador on board. From my connection to Voices Against Trafficking™, I had come to know about the Airline Ambassador program, which allows partnerships with the airline industry to help vulnerable children, using airline employees and others who "travel to make a difference," as leading advocates for awareness of human trafficking prevention in the aviation industry.

On the walk down the jetty, I decided to duck into the first empty seat available and get the steward's attention. Coincidence would have it; I caught the attention of the head stewardess who sat near me just before takeoff. I told her hurriedly that I had concerns someone might be trafficking a child on this flight. Before I said anything else, she described the man in detail and gave a brief description of the child. "I noticed him as soon as he came aboard," she replied. I was so relieved that I sank back into the first-class seat and breathed a sigh.

A few minutes later, as they were pushing back from the gate, she said she got his name from the manifest, identified his seat, and would follow up with me after takeoff. The emotional rollercoaster I had been on for the past half hour wore me out. After texting my allies in the anti-trafficking fight, I dozed off. As we were making our final descent, the stewardess woke me.

"I spoke to him," she began. "I think he is just a normal new father."

I don't know if her words reassured her own conscience, but they did not satisfy mine. I remained silent but gave her a puzzled look.

"He said her name is Isabella Rose," she said after a momentary pause.

"Don't you think it is odd that he told you her full name?" I questioned.

"No," she said quickly. "I can follow him when he gets off the plane to make sure he doesn't do anything. Or you can follow him." Follow him? Why not have a SWAT team waiting for a formal inquiry? Am I really going to follow a 290-pound man who may or may not be involved in human trafficking? Moreover, am I doing this in the nation's busiest airport at midnight?

When we landed in Atlanta, I was the first one off the plane. I high-tailed it to the police department located in the baggage claim area to file a report. Their office was empty, but a phone number was taped to the door for assistance. No one answered on my first, second, or third try. I went to the TSA in Atlanta and asked where I could file a report. I was told that it was a police matter, not a TSA matter. Outside, at curbside check-in, police officers were always directing traffic. That was my next stop. But oddly enough, it must have been a shift change, because no one was around. I went back to TSA after swinging by our baggage carousel to see if he was there.

After a brief exchange with the two TSA agents, I ended our conversation with a shocking revelation: The entire Hartsfield-Jackson Atlanta airport is completely unsecured from traffickers and most other assailants. We were sitting ducks. Our airports are porous and easily breached, even in a post-9/11 America. I couldn't believe the opportunity for crime I was witnessing.

If there is a handoff, I thought, at least I could take another photo and upload it to the anti-trafficking database. But there was no other photo to be had. The man never showed up at the baggage carousel to get the child's car seat because there was none. No luggage for him, no car seat for her, nothing but a diaper bag with store tags on it and a baby dressed like a Christmas present.

Isabella Rose, are you okay? Is that even your real name? For those who remain unnamed, what are we going to do to stop the slave trade on our shores? *Where is their emancipation?*

WorldsChildren.org reports that 27% of trafficking victims are children. The 2020 Trafficking In Persons (TIP) report from the U.S. Department of State points out that the instability and lack of access to critical services caused by the pandemic have made more people vulnerable to exploitation. Traffickers have capitalized on that instability, adjusting their business models to the "new normal," reminding us all that human trafficking isn't going anywhere.

Dr. Lisa Babbage, PhD has been involved with a variety of causes all aimed at restoring women and children through education, needs-based support, and workforce development. After twenty years in the classroom, and over ten years in the mission field of Atlanta, Lisa says her work has only just begun.She is a Charter member of Voices Against Trafficking™, and works to provide temporary housing for at-risk women in her city through her own nonprofit Maranatha House. She is the author of over twenty books, most of which are focused on restoration, and is a documentary filmmaker. In 2020, she became an Emancipation Brand Ambassador for COL1972 and spokesperson for GAE Coalition.

FILMMAKING AND FAITH – PARTNERING TO END HUMAN TRAFFICKING

By Andi Buerger, JD

———

Most children under the age of five are not too concerned with their futures, if they even think past "today" at all. But Travis Conover was not your average youngster. At age four, Travis boldly told his family that he was going to be on television someday so that he could make people happy. Today, Travis's life brings a living truth to the vision and unwavering conviction he had as a child.

"I never fit the traditional mold. I grew up in a small town near Albany, New York. The population was maybe twenty-five people. Basically, you worked a 9-to-5 job or went to school, came home, and played in the dirt. That was the culture."

Born in Red Bank, New Jersey, Travis moved to upstate New York as an infant and lived what seemed like a caged life. He always felt like a big fish in a small pond, keeping his desire to become an actor locked up inside. Surrounded by small-town culture, such desires just didn't fit. At the age of fourteen, Travis got a break and moved to Saratoga Springs, New York. Saratoga

Springs was a much bigger pond that offered bigger opportunities.

Travis became a wrestler and managed—barely—to graduate from high school. "I just never connected with a *traditional* learning environment. I was creative. I hated sitting in a classroom for eight hours a day staring at a chalkboard. I went to college and flunked out. I honestly went because I thought it was 'the right thing to do'—so that's what I did."

In tenth grade, a friend told Travis about a martial arts school that was offering two free weeks of Taekwondo classes. When Travis went home and told his mother, she was not as excited as Travis was about the opportunity. She was adamantly opposed because she knew he had tried many things before and had a track record of not following through. Despite her concerns, she gave her son one last chance to try something and stick to it. Travis and three friends decided to take the free Taekwondo classes.

After only three short months, Master Brian Miller saw something unique in Travis. Based on the support and leadership Travis was receiving from Master Miller, Travis quickly became an assistant Taekwondo instructor. The discipline of martial arts and Master Miller's ongoing mentorship helped mold Travis's teen and early adult years. Master Miller's integrity impacted Travis's confidence and direction at a very impressionable time in his life.

Within six months, Travis began teaching new students. At just seventeen, young Travis was teaching classes full-time to students ranging from "little dragons" all the way up to the sixty-plus set.

Remarkably, Travis achieved his red belt at eighteen years old, and his achievements led him to compete in regional tournaments. But he wanted to do something bigger, something more creative with his art form. During a regional competition, he started thinking about creating a board break he had never seen before. That same month, he taught himself how to do a backflip. He decided he was going to win the competition by successfully backflipping over a board and breaking it on the way down. He did, and he won.

As a result of that particular competition, Travis drew the attention of Master Adam Grogin. Master Grogin wanted to recruit Travis to become part of Team Pil-Sung, and he respectfully asked Master Miller if he could do so. Team Pil-Sung is an elite martial arts team comprised of martial artists from different styles, schools, and specialties. It specializes in modern martial arts theatrical and action performance as well as traditional and modern martial arts competition. Team Pil-Sung is where Travis's performance career began. Under the expert leadership of Master Adam Grogin, he quickly became a captain with this extraordinary team.

During the four years that Travis toured with Team Pil-Sung, a film and television college approached Master Adam Grogin about a project. Team Pil-Sung members were praised for their extraordinary performance skills. So much so that the New School of Radio and Television in Albany, New York, wanted some of the Team Pil-Sung members to make a movie with them, specifically Travis. Master Grogin knew intuitively that film acting was where Travis really belonged. Travis was cast in a leading role for the thesis project, *Martial*, an action short film.

At the end of the college film college, Travis found himself at an emotional crossroads. This experience had awakened a passion that had been dormant in him for many years. He *knew*, without a doubt, that making movies was all he ever wanted to do. For so many years, he had felt like it would be impossible, but with God placing breadcrumbs at his feet, he felt for the first time that maybe, *just maybe,* it could really happen.

Soon after, God opened doors for Travis to start his own martial arts school in Oneonta, NY. He named it Jin Shil Martial Arts, meaning "The Way of Truth." Travis moved in with his father, who helped him start teaching martial arts classes in the basement of his church. Travis's good friends, Joe and Shirley Rufrano, signed up for classes and helped him recruit others to enroll. Eventually, Travis's father helped him get a space in a strip mall to hold the classes. With enrollment growing by the class, Jin Shil Martial Arts became the biggest martial arts school in town. The success of his business created the opportunity for Travis to begin buying up other martial arts schools in the area.

Travis was not just a known name in the business community; he was also someone who gave back. As a martial arts instructor, his students and their parents often asked him for advice. Travis willingly shared sound counsel and his own life experiences to help others. Though not a professional counselor, he enjoyed helping kids do better in school and watching struggling couples find their way to a better place as a result of his interactions with them. Like teachers, doctors, and many more in positions of authority whom others come to trust, Travis provided more than just martial arts classes: he invited patrons to be part of a community family.

The content of Travis's character and his successes along the way brought new opportunities that would continue to refine both his heart's desire to be an actor and the direction to take to accomplish this dream. One direction came through Joe and Shirley, who had been good friends of Travis's for some time. A few years into their own martial arts journey, the couple invited

Travis to speak at a young entrepreneurs conference. Travis spoke on the topic of courage, sharing that courage was a formula of knowledge plus practice.

In that same conference, there were break-out rooms where facilitators asked people about their dreams and what they really wanted to do with their lives. They shared an illustration called the rocking chair test. The rocking chair test asks participants to picture themselves sitting in a rocking chair on a quiet porch and to imagine looking back on their own life. From the perspective of hindsight, each participant reflects on what was most important. A facilitator poses this challenge to participants: "Ask yourself, have I done everything in my life that I really wanted to do and had to do? Do I feel totally fulfilled in my dreams and purpose?" Each participant thinks about whether they are proud of the decisions they made and actions they took or if they would choose differently given another chance at life.

Three months before the young entrepreneurs' conference, Travis had actually been struggling with his desire to become an actor. It was so intense that it would keep him up at night. He couldn't shake it anymore. It burned like a fire in his heart. He cried out to God, "Is this what you want me to do?" Travis knew the desire and the direction had to be from God, or it would be impossible to accomplish.

As Travis listened to the same conference attendees who had *just heard him speak* about courage, he knew he had something to say–and that it would most likely shock the attendees. Preparing to "practice" courage in front of everyone in the room, he stood up. Boldly, he announced: "I *need* to be an actor." Silence filled the room. After a few moments, Travis's friend Sam put his arm around him in approval and exclaimed, "Man! I can't wait to see you on the big screen!" Travis was just as shocked as everyone else. Shocked and relieved. He knew then that he had to speak with his dad.

Travis and his dad met in short order. He told his dad that he wanted to leave his successful martial arts business, including the use of the strip mall that his dad had helped to arrange when Travis needed a new location for his school. After hearing the news, to Travis's surprise, his dad answered, "I know you have to go. God's got this. We'll figure it out." He was equally surprised to learn that God had given his dad a dream about Travis needing to leave the martial arts school and head in a different direction. It was in this special father-son moment that Travis's dad shared that he had had the dream *three months before* the young entrepreneurs' conference. Travis's dad knew *before Travis did* that God had a different path for his son to follow, one that Travis got a glimpse of when he was only four years old.

Travis scheduled a meeting with the biggest martial arts school in the area. He offered to sell his business to the owner at a price that was less than ideal but enough to move Travis to New Jersey. The owner agreed, and it proved to be perfect timing. One of Travis's students worked for a producer who needed a martial artist model for a Ralph Lauren spot. Travis ended up getting the spot. From there, modeling, small acting gigs, and commercials filled his time.

While overnight success didn't happen, God provided more bread crumbs along the way. After two years of acting, Travis realized that he needed professional training, so he enrolled himself in acting school while working his other gigs. One of the things Travis soon learned on his journey was that many people in the modeling and fashion industries are *not* who they say they are. Sometimes, it is more like a room of mirrors. You never really know who's behind each mirror.

Not long after Travis started professional acting classes, another breadcrumb arrived and bumped his career up another level. Bruce Weber, the fashion director who had given Travis his first modeling gig, told Travis that he loved his work. Weber was doing a new campaign for Versace and wanted Travis to work for him. The campaign would need Travis for three days at a pay rate of several thousand dollars per day, plus expenses and luxury hotel accommodations.

Travis enjoyed the project immensely and ended up working with Donatella Versace herself. The burning desire within the up-and-coming actor made every other free moment during that modeling gig a chance to find more work. Travis reached out to a director and provided his acting reel. Director Mike Saint Gerard actually came to Travis's hotel room—the one Versace had provided—and auditioned Travis on the spot for a new short film he was directing. Travis nailed it.

Gerard could see that *who* Travis was as a man of God was even more impressive than his acting chops. He cast Travis to play a co-starring role in his short film, *The Trial of Everett Mann*.

Travis worked hard to please his director, who preferred method acting, something that went against both Travis's classical training and his nature in general. Method acting is an emotion-oriented technique, while classical acting is primarily action-based. The short film won several awards throughout some of the largest film festivals in the world, including the very prestigious Cannes Film Festival. Shortly after his on-screen acting debut in *The Trial Of Everett Mann*, Travis booked an acting and producing role in *The Penitent Thief* (featuring actor Kevin Sorbo), which hit theaters during the Easter season of 2020. With his career progressing upwards, Travis signed with one of the best agencies in the southeast: J Pervis Talent.

A few years later, Travis met Shannon, his future wife, at a business conference in San Diego. They discovered on their first date that they each had a heart to help human trafficking victims. Shannon had been in an abusive twenty-year marriage and had nine children of her own already. In spite of her circumstances, Shannon single-handedly built a successful business and positioned herself to break out of the situation she had been forced into for so many years. When they married, Travis became an instant stepdad to nine children! Since then, the happy couple have added three more boys to their family, bringing the total number of Conover kids to twelve. As Travis said, "I am *very* passionate about children!"

In 2022, Travis connected with a man named J. Matthew "Matt" Wallace, a successful actor and producer, at a church in Atlanta. Their paths had crossed a few times at church over the years, but finally had a chance to connect on a deeper level and discuss working together. Travis had become frustrated with experiences he had encountered in a number of acting groups, so he decided to start his own. Travis opened up his home to actors wanting to refine their craft with other like-minded artists. Unlike other acting groups, Travis did not charge actors to join. Matt found out about Travis's acting group and got involved. It wasn't long before Matt and Travis realized that they were more aligned then they first had realized. Matt was impressed with Travis's skill and work ethic on top of his dedicated faith in God. Travis felt the same, reflecting that Matt was both a great actor and a phenomenal man of God. The two men decided together that God had brought them together in friendship for a reason.

Like millions of others who saw the movie *Taken*, Travis became more aware and passionate about the issue of human trafficking. He knew that the taking of innocent children, in particular, to be sold for profit was real. The truth burned within him as he researched what is known today as twenty-first-century slavery. His passion to "do something" to bring greater awareness to this issue and help victims grew slowly over time.

During the pandemic years, the film industry basically shut down. Travis was itching to film something and create. "It's not that I just want to… I *have* to." He just hadn't landed on what story to tell. He did, however, have a scene in his head for a short film, like a piece of a movie that rolled around in his mind for three or four years. He envisioned a story of a rescue mission, getting a victim back from human traffickers using either the military or independent rescuers. But he only had one scene in his mind.

Travis decided to call Matt to ask if he would do a project with him. Travis hadn't written anything, but he knew there was a story there somewhere. Matt agreed. Now, the hunt for the story began. At three o'clock one morning, Travis woke up with a story filling his mind. He immediately said to himself, "I know what I want to do!"

He ran downstairs to start writing. In less than an hour, he wrote a thirteen-page script. Travis wasted no time pitching it to Matt. Travis envisioned an episodic—short episodes that, when edited together at the end of the season, would create a feature film. Matt hadn't read any of Travis's previous work, so as was usual, Matt approached the script with caution. A bit of a perfectionist, Matt is known for having a keen eye for quality content. After reading Travis's first episode, Matt called to report, "Hey… This is actually really good!"

While Travis originally considered making a web series, he had to get the first episode filmed. The challenge was that he had no money to do it. Travis called in favors from various people to get the episode put together and directed and edited it himself to save money. When all was said and done, industry professionals praised the actors involved as "top-notch" talent.

For Travis, it was good, but not good enough. He realized that the message needed to be bigger. Today, Travis continues his quest to make a greater impact in communities worldwide through film and other entertainment projects.

Andi Buerger, JD is Founder of Voices Against Trafficking™. Her books *Voices Against Trafficking™ - The Strength of Many Voices Speaking As One* and *A Fragile Thread of Hope: One Survivor's Quest to Rescue* are available on Amazon.com. Her *Voices of Courage* magazine is available online at *Voices of Courage*.media with a television program, also titled *Voices of Courage*, due out in 2026. Andi's work continues to appear in numerous publications, books, online news outlets, and bestselling titles including *Everyday Triumph - Extraordinary Stories of Hope, Resilience, and Impact,* by Chris Meek, Ed.D.

UGANDA: PREVENTION AND RESPONSE TO TRAFFICKING IN PERSONS

By Detective Nusura Kemigisha

———

Uganda is a source, transit, and destination country for the vice of trafficking in persons, both domestically and transnationally.

According to Uganda's Annual Crime Report dated 2022, 668 cases of trafficking in persons were registered, compared to 421 cases registered in 2021. The more recent figure may seem like a questionable increase, but it is important to note most trafficking in persons cases were previously filed as other offenses such as rape, assault, child abuse, and kidnapping, among others. This has been due to law enforcement officers' limited awareness and identification of the elements of human trafficking. Increased training by the Uganda Police Force, Uganda's Human Trafficking Institute, and other stakeholders has led to an increase in cases reported nationwide.

The Prevention of Trafficking in Persons Act (2009) is used when it comes to charging perpetrators of this crime, in addition to other laws depending on the available evidence.

There are various forms of human exploitation, such as sexual, labor, organ harvesting, and child marriage, as well as harmful cultural practices, such as female genital mutilation, ritual child sacrifices, and forced begging. In Uganda, these offenses are recognized as "Trafficking in Persons" and are punishable by law based on the details or elements of the crime.

In an effort to address these offenses, the Uganda Police Force officially established the Anti-Trafficking in Persons Department under the Criminal Investigations Directorate in 2019. This dedicated team of police officers has been specially trained on how to manage cases with a victim-centered approach.

The Uganda Police Force established thirteen Anti-Trafficking in Persons Task Forces at major border districts. These police officers are trained to identify both victims and suspects of trafficking in persons. They carry out assessments and investigate cases throughout the judicial process. In addition, dedicated officers are posted at each district police station, manned by a well-trained detective with knowledge of prevention and response to trafficking in persons cases.

Uganda Police has several ongoing capacity-building initiatives and partnerships with key stakeholders, including the criminal justice system, the Human Trafficking Institute, Operation Underground Railroad, UNODC, and others.

In a joint effort, Uganda has organized and operates a transitional shelter for victims of trafficking. In 2022, this facility hosted over 440 victims and is well-equipped with a child-friendly space and interview room. Based on needs assessment, victims are immediately accommodated upon rescue and referred to other stakeholders for more support on a case-by-case basis. It is worth noting that the primary goal of the national task force is to assist victims and prosecute offenders.

Despite these efforts, a number of challenges among the police and other key actors have hindered the prevention and prosecution of human trafficking. One of these challenges is a limited awareness of the forms, nature, and magnitude of the crime in Uganda. Citizens are not aware of the manifestations of trafficking and, in most cases, easily become victims or aid perpetrators in committing this crime.

The second challenge is the limited technical and financial capacity in the investigations of these cases through the judicial process. These cases often have a number of crime scenes due to the movement of victims and suspects from one place to another. Coordinating these efforts from the place of origin, transit, and destination creates an added challenge and prolongs the investigations. Thirdly, most victims are not cooperative when it comes to prosecuting offenders. They are key witnesses but cannot be compelled to give testimony in court.

Despite these challenges, the Uganda Police, in close partnership with the Director of Public Prosecution, have made significant achievements in the prevention and prosecution of human trafficking. Prosecutors work alongside officers as they gather evidence and prepare for trial to ensure they are handling each case in a victim-centered way.

Uganda has worked tirelessly to improve its trafficking response and has celebrated major successes in convicting traffickers and protecting victims throughout the country.

Nusura Kemigisha is Detective Assistant Superintendent of Uganda Police. She is also Deputy Head Sexual and Children Offenses Department and Criminal Investigations Directorate in the Uganda Police Force.

WHOLESOME TO HYPERSEXUALIZED: WHAT HAPPENED TO CHILDREN'S DANCE?

By Mary Margaret Bawden

There has been a cultural shift from healthy, educational children's dance to harmful, hypersexualized children's dance at younger and younger ages. The art of children's dance has been hijacked.

Mary Bawden was a little girl who wanted to dance.

I dreamed about it. All the time. I begged my mother for lessons. All the time. But we moved six times in my first twelve years of life. My parents were always changing schools, churches, doctors, and dentists for me and my three other siblings. Investigating dance was not on the priority list. So the begging continued.

When I finally started ballet at eleven years of age, the lessons aligned with my dreams. Through movement, I felt a healthy change inside my heart that integrated mind, body, and spirit. That produced in me what the overwhelming research reveals about the art of dance for children: improved cognitive and academic development, confidence, creativity, relational maturity, and so much more[2].

It should be no surprise that dance became an integral part of my identity. After I completed high school, I received a Bachelor of Arts in modern dance from the University of California at Riverside and a Master of Arts degree in worship with an emphasis in dance from Hope International University in Fullerton, California. Those degrees supported the church dance ministry I led for over twenty years. Movement was a joy. Actually, it became worship. I even wrote a book[3] about it.

Sometime along the way, I started to notice a cultural shift in the art form of dance. It came gradually, with no definitive boundaries. A quiet, silent darkness began to distort dance. I was particularly disturbed by how it impacted children. Without realizing it, the dance environment went from healthy, educational children's dance to harmful, hypersexualized children's dance with adult costumes, choreography, and music. It continues to occur with children of younger and younger ages.

While the positive research outcomes for healthy, holistic educational children's dance are clear, the APA research outcomes[4] for harmful, hypersexualized children's dance indicates lifelong pathology. They range from depression and poor aca-

---

[2] Edel Quin and Emma Redding, "The health benefits of creative dance: Improving children's physical and psychological wellbeing," *ResearchGate*, last modified January 2007, accessed April 14, 2022, https://www.researchgate.net/publication/288511877_The_health_benefits_of_creative_dance_Improving_children's_physical_and_psychological_wellbeing.

[3] Mary Bawden, *Dance is Prayer in Motion: Soul to Sole Choreography for Christian Dance Ministry,* (Amazon, Advantage Books, 2016)

[4] "Report of the APA Task Force on the Sexualization of Girls," *American Psychology Association*, accessed April 14, 2022, https://www.apa.org/pi/women/programs/girls/report.

demic performance to body dysmorphia and eating disorders, early pregnancy, a higher risk of abusive relationships, porn objectification, and the promotion of a rape culture.

Physical and emotional injury from hypersexualized children's dance also extends to abusive internet connections. Harmful dance has led online predators to contact dance students when they post dance videos from their classes on unfiltered social media platforms. The national spotlight on the growth of hypersexualized dance grooms children for future relationship abuse[5]. Why? Because children copy what they see. Brain research[6] refers to this process as "mirror neurons." It is a key aspect of child development. Moreover, children who are exposed to adult sexual material experience neurological stress. Their brains are simply not mature enough to handle the exposure to adult sexual material. They are also more likely to develop impulsive behavior and less able to think critically. Not only does this affect brain development, but it leads to trauma outcomes from PTSD[7] (post-traumatic stress disorder) to ACE[8] (adverse childhood experience).

Last but not least, the research[9] shows that adults who watch hypersexualized children in dance see that child as someone not

---

5   "Grooming and Red Flag Behaviors," *Darkness to Light*, accessed April 14, 2022, https://www.d2l.org/child-grooming-signs-behavior-awareness/.
6   Kristen Jenson, "Can Soft-Core Porn Damage Your Child's Brain?", accessed April 14, 2022, http://protectyoungminds.org/2014/09/04/can-soft-core-porn-damage-your-childs-brain/.
7   B.D. Perry, "Neurobiological sequelae of childhood trauma: PTSD in children" in *Catecholamine Function in Posttraumatic Stress Disorder: Emerging Concepts*. M. Michele Murburg (American Psychiatric Association, 1994), pp. 233–255.
8   "Adverse Childhood Experiences (ACEs)," *Centers for Disease Control and Prevention*, accessed April 14, 2022, https://www.cdc.gov/violenceprevention/aces/index.html.
9   Elise Holland and Nick Haslam, "Sexualised girls are seen as less intelligent and less worthy of help than their peers," *The Conversation*, accessed April 14,

deserving dignity, lacking an independent mind, and unintelligent. That has made it easy to dehumanize a child, commodify them, and be violent toward them. It's a perfect storm. Low cultural awareness of inappropriate media exposure coupled with corporate financial greed is center stage. Researcher Philip Adams has coined the term "corporate paedophilia[10]" to describe how we use children to make money for adults.

"Corporate paedophilia is a metaphor that describes the selling of products to children before they are able to understand advertising, and thus before they are able to consent to the process of corporate-led consumption. The metaphor draws a parallel between actual paedophilia, the use of children for the sexual pleasure of adults, and corporate use of children for the financial benefit of adults who own and manage corporations."

All of these harmful dance factors work to normalize what is not normal. It's a complicated story founded on inappropriate exposure to adult sexual issues and a culture taken by surprise. Several years ago, I started on my own personal journey of education and awareness.

As an adult choreographer, I taught a little girl healthy dance. After she grew up, I was encouraged to attend her student-led college dance concert. Initially, I was thrilled to go; then I became disturbed. Instead of art, I saw hypersexualized dance accompanied by catcalls from men during the two-hour concert. I hoped it was an aberration. When I attended the concert the next year, I expected to see different choreography, costumes,

---

2022, https://theconversation.com/sexualised-girls-are-seen-as-less-intelligent-and-less-worthy-of-help-than-their-peers-46537.

10 Emma Rush and Andrea La Nauze, "Corporate Paedophilia Sexualisation of children in Australia," *The Australia Institute*, accessed April 14, 2022 https://australiainstitute.org.au/wp-content/uploads/2020/12/DP90_8.pdf.

and music, but I was shocked. That concert was even more disturbing. By the way, that program did not resemble anything that had been a part of my university dance education or any personal dance experience. I was deeply grieved to see women choosing self-objectification with adult costumes, choreography, and music, but, after all, these were adult college students over 18 years of age. That silenced my soul, until…

I saw the same kinds of dances in high school dance concerts, junior high dance concerts, elementary school dance concerts…and then in the preschool classes. It was a nightmare that came to life. If you peek into my heart, you'll understand why I founded DA:NCE (Dance Awareness: No Child Exploited). As a dance educator and caring adult who experienced the joy of healthy dance, I felt, and continue to feel, a need to educate others about this dangerous trend so that we might protect children and protect the art of dance. There is a huge difference between healthy and harmful dance. The differences need to be defined so that people can make informed choices.

Let's take a minute to read a personal story of harmful dance that matches what the research shows. Let me introduce you to Danielle Freitag. She is a licensed counselor, author, and CEO of Action169[11], an organization that offers holistic restoration services for women who've experienced exploitation. Danielle bravely shares her story of overcoming commercial sexual exploitation, which was influenced by learning hypersexualized dance.

"As a little girl, I loved to sing and dance. At first, I would twirl around the house like a ballerina without ever thinking I needed to have anyone to dance with, or for.

---

11 Action169, accessed April 14, 2022, https://www.Action169.com.

Like so many young girls, I had taken years of dance lessons—jazz, tap, and ballet. I distinctly remember the years prior to being able to wear pointe shoes, also known as toe shoes. Readiness to begin pointe work depended on strength, technique, attitude, and even commitment. Ballet classes were weekly, and it didn't take long before I was in pointe shoes. I recall practicing demi pliés in the studio, at home, and really anywhere I went.

As a young girl, there was innocence in the way that I moved. To be able to move freely in expressions that elicit beauty offered a sense of liveliness that connected me with beauty and delicacy. I've always loved to dance. Whether choreographed or free-style, dance was something enjoyable for me.

Over a progression of time, what was once innocent became compromised. What I did not know in the younger years of my life, was that the hypersexualized dance I was taught was linked to a grooming process that would make way for my entrance into the commercial sex industry.

Even though I learned mostly age-appropriate dance choreography in a studio as a young girl, the same place I learned ballet, I also learned from the music videos, movies, and the clubs I wasn't old enough to be in.

Movies like *Dirty Dancing* captured my attention. Watching the dancing, both the appropriate and sexualized dance, taught me ways to move my body. With the purest of motives, my dear grandmother would fast-forward through the scenes with *dirty* dancing as she rightfully believed that seeing people dance provocatively would teach my young mind a kind of inappropriate behavior.

Eventually, I saw the entire movie, learning that there were other forms of dance than what I'd known.

Unintentionally seeing pornography at a young age was also a pivotal moment of influence. Seeing people posing in pictures without their clothes on in the same body behaviors I was seeing in the culture of compromised dance was confusing, yet an aspect of grooming. The older boyfriend, who instructed me to remove my clothes as a teenager and perform a "harmless striptease," also had an influence.

In fact, he was the one who brought me into the strip club industry, where dance was completely seductive and for one purpose–arousal. Pivotal moments, including learning seductive body movements, exploited my vulnerabilities. The grooming process taught me my worth as a body commodity meant to put on a show.

At first, my entrance into the strip club industry was exhilarating, somehow empowering, and even glamorous. It was all a facade. Eventually, I saw the industry for everything that it is: exploitative, disempowering, and destructive. My body on a stage, once a little girl with hopes and dreams who danced like a ballerina, now dancing in seductive movements for all to see. I wasn't singing anymore, and I certainly wasn't dancing the way I once did. After five years of working as an exotic dancer, the fancy term for *stripper*, I wasn't creating anything of beauty or innocence. I wanted out. I was tired of seductive dance.

Seductive dance is meant to draw the viewer into a performance that produces arousal. The Latin origin of the word 'seduction' means to lead, or attempt to lead, astray, enchant, or entice into a wrong or foolish course, especially a sexual act. The dancing styles of seduction are many, including alluring, tantalizing, and charming. Movements with an emphasis on articulations of the hips, butt, or breasts used to punctuate the music or accent a beat are sexualized movements reminding the viewer of sex, which is why these movements cause arousal.

Bouncier movements of appropriated twerking or grinding movements certainly have no place in public dance and, especially, in children's dance. The sexualization of children and young teens in the culture, and especially in dance classes, is completely inappropriate.

Hypersexualized movements imposed on small children who don't understand what they're doing is a form of grooming that sets them up into a pornified culture that places value on the body for seduction. Teaching seductive dance to young girls grooms them into the lie that there is power in being commodified."

Commodification has nothing to do with a child's best interests and everything to do with making money for the porn industry, media platforms, and online or in-person predators. Danielle's story represents a cultural tsunami. **Children deserve** to learn and experience the gift of dance in safe environments that do not sexualize and/or exploit them. **Children deserve** to love dance, their bodies, and themselves. **Children deserve** to be protected from sexual exploitation.

Let's get to work. To clarify the process and keep you current about the differences between healthy and harmful dance, use these simplified definitions to educate others:

- Healthy dance: In healthy dance, which equals educational dance, *children look like children* and are dressed in age-appropriate costumes, using age-appropriate choreography and music, usually accompanied by a wonderful sense of joy.
- Harmful dance: In harmful dance, which equals hypersexualized dance, *children look like adults* and are dressed

in adult costumes, using adult choreography and music, usually accompanied by adult hairstyles and makeup.

Remember, children are not mini-adults. *They are children* who need time and space to develop physically, mentally, and emotionally. So, what is the solution to stop the hypersexualization of children with adult costumes, choreography, and music? How can we engage in protecting children but not get overwhelmed? The issue itself is complicated, but the solution isn't. Below are practical steps that you can share in your relational world with the adults around you. *It happens one person at a time.*

1. Identify the problem with awareness. *We can't address what we don't have the courage to name.* Understand the differences between healthy and harmful dance.
2. Make informed choices.
3. Educate adults with practical tools from DA:NCE on danceawareness.com: newsletter, ebook, short videos, trailers, presentations, and research. All materials are free.
4. Understand that YOU are the protective factor for children in dance. YOU are the "take action" prevention. WE are the key to preventing grooming and abuse in children's dance because we are the adults who supervise the choice of dance studios, children's access to the internet, and their exposure to inappropriate media. You should be informed that this trend is not necessarily related to the dance industry. Many uninformed parents in all cultural categories are pressuring dance studios to hypersexualize children.

As you educate others about this topic (and join the DA:NCE Team), it's helpful to understand the four educational goals of

DA:NCE. I've listed them below. They provide the "why" of what DA:NCE does:
1. To protect children from hypersexualization in adult costumes, choreography, and music, and to protect the art of dance
2. To create free research materials to give adults informed choices about the differences between healthy or harmful dance
3. To engage in respectful conversations about hypersexualization without shaming/demonizing adults or dance studios so that there is a path for reflection and changed perspectives
4. To communicate the hypersexualization of children in dance and its connection to the public health issue of pornography with bipartisan engagement

Join me in the journey to protect children and protect the art of dance. Visit danceawareness.com to engage your mind, heart, and body with the tools to overcome a dangerous trend. Take note: this trend affects all children, not just children taking dance lessons. I'm going to repeat that: **It affects all children, not just children taking dance lessons.**

All children are being exposed to a pornified culture. The solution to hypersexualized children's dance is NOT solved by taking kids out of dance. Research shows that harmful dance impacts children whether they dance or not because of the ongoing media exposure to the porn industry. Remember that healthy dance is a wonderful activity for children of all ages (and adults too). Actually, the solution to harmful dance is healthy dance, because research shows that healthy dance engages the mind, body, and spirit: the whole person. That's how we need to see every child: a whole human who needs caring adults to navigate a complicated culture.

Mary Bawden, Author
DA:NCE Awareness: No Child Exploited
www.danceawareness.com

Danielle Freitag, LADC, **Contributor**
Author, Co-founding Executive Director of Action169
www.action169.com

ACTRESS ANNE HECHE – CRAZY? A SURVIVOR SPEAKS OUT

By Andi Buerger, JD

Many people thought Anne Heche was crazy, a privileged eccentric. The press well documented her wild ups and downs and bouts of mental illness. Eccentric? She had been a successful actress with a colorful love life, most notably and publicly her relationship with Ellen DeGeneres. Her journey included a couple of marriages and two children. But she was also known for strange claims and unpredictable behavior in interviews. Was she crazy? Was the odd behavior fueled by substance abuse? My belief is yes—and no. What the public and entertainment influencers did not know was the little-known *root* of what drove Anne Heche's very erratic behavior. I knew. As a survivor, I understood it all too well. I too was a victim of familial sexual abuse.

I understood the secrets and suffering that led Anne Heche to create an alter ego. Only a survivor of childhood abuse can comprehend the need to find some way to survive the violent physical attack an innocent child suffers from familial abuse. Fantasy worlds and alter egos are common methods used by young victims to live through it. According to an interview in 2001 on ABC, "Heche stated that she created a fantasy world called the 'Fourth Dimension' to make herself feel safe and had an alter ego who was the daughter of God and half-sister of Jesus Christ named Celestia." It was a form of self-protection to hide her shame and suffering.

Her battle was to survive and live beyond her childhood trauma and the haunting memories. Sadly, Heche could never escape them. Her tragedy was that she could not beat the devil. She could not obliterate the horror she suffered as a child. She could not overcome the mental scars of that brutality and did not achieve healing or freedom to live authentically as herself: Anne Heche.

I am the lucky one. I survived *seventeen* years as a child sex trafficking victim, where immediate and extended family members leveled unspeakable abuse and torture. In my life, God interceded. I tried to end my life three separate times before the age of twelve, but no one knew. Going to school was my "safe place" away from family predators, but I never stopped wondering if, at any moment, someone would find out, someone would know what I was hiding inside. It was a heavy load for a child to carry.

Each day was another day of self-loathing, fear, and hopeless desperation. Like Heche's family, my family worked hard to control the fake image everyone else saw – often through force and public humiliation. Family predators are "protected" by their bloodline. Child victims have no escape – nor any advocates. I wanted to hurt myself to stop the gnawing shame and pain of my filthy past and all its secrets. I wished I could be anyone *but me*. Like Heche, I was trained to be the perfect pretender. Decades later, I achieved a healthier, more authentic self that allowed me to live forward, live freely, and prevent shame demons from defeating me.

I developed excellent coping skills and put on a game face in public, which made it possible for me to operate in any situation, including work, church, and unhealthy relationships. However, my game face did not fill the void in my identity. None of it made me feel whole, human, or worthy. It was my faith in God that sustained me. This faith, effective counseling, and a deep calling in my heart to reach other young victims who have been violated, abused, and often abandoned—even by their own families.

Anne Heche sought out healing and to see good in her life. Her battle was made more difficult because there are so many, including medical professionals, who do not know how to effectively help a victim of such depravity. Why does this ignorance still exist, considering the multitudes of victims of child abuse and human trafficking? Combating that lack of awareness is a key tenet of Voices Against Trafficking™ (VAT), a 501(c)3 entity I founded to heighten public awareness about violence against children, especially, in the United States and also abroad. The cost of collective ignorance is immeasurable. Its long-term effects on our nation's future are irreversible.

Anne Heche's death was a casualty of the war against the innocent. The truth is that she was a victim of familial child sex abuse. She lost her fight against the evil forced upon her by those who should have loved and protected her. May her life and death be a rallying point for those who are fighting against predators and human traffickers. Each member of Congress, law enforcement, educational institutions, medical and mental health care communities, civil rights advocacy centers, and every community needs to join in the effort to stop the abuse against our children. The most innocent among us deserve to have their human rights and dignity protected.

Anne Heche created a courageous image throughout the violence and shame she endured. Honoring her is honoring all victims.

For more information, visit Voices Against Trafficking™ (VoicesAgainstTrafficking.com).

Andi Buerger, JD is Founder of Voices Against Trafficking™. Her books *Voices Against Trafficking™ - The Strength of Many Voices Speaking As One* and *A Fragile Thread of Hope: One Survivor's Quest to Rescue* are available on Amazon.com. Her *Voices of Courage* magazine is available online at *Voices of Courage*.media with a television program, also titled *Voices of Courage*, due out in 2026. Andi's work continues to appear in numerous publications, books, online news outlets, and bestselling titles including *Everyday Triumph - Extraordinary Stories of Hope, Resilience, and Impact*, by Chris Meek, Ed.D.

PROTECTING EVERYDAY PEOPLE FROM EVERYDAY THREATS

By Hunter Allen

No one should ever be a victim of physical violence. Yet every day in our country, that is exactly what happens to many innocent people.

My name is Hunter Allen. I am a self-defense expert, master self-defense instructor, and bodyguard. At the age of eleven, I started training in martial arts and have never stopped. I'm sixty-three and live every day of my life in the service of others. Because of this, I can teach people how to realistically defend themselves against any and all violent attacks.

Briefly, let me tell you about my decision to learn how to defend myself. At six years of age, my mother gave me up for adoption. At that moment, I went from being a happy boy with a brother and two sisters to living with strangers. The people I ended up with molested me and beat me relentlessly, and I learned to live in constant fear. Then, at age nine, I was raped by a neighbor. To survive, I learned to shut my mouth and do what I was told. I also learned to submit and let people use my body for their pleasure.

When I was eleven, I asked the people I lived with if I could learn martial arts. They said if I paid my own way, they would allow me to learn. I cut lawns, delivered newspapers, washed cars, and whatever else I could do to pay for my training. I never looked back and have never stopped training. Throughout the years, I constantly found myself standing up to protect anyone around me who needed my help. I wanted to do more, and I knew I could!

I started to train others and developed a training syllabus to allow anyone to defend themselves instantly, effectively, and safely against any physical violence so they would never become a victim. At my school, TIG Tactical, I teach my students how to survive against any and all threats: bigger, faster, stronger, armed or unarmed opponents, or even multiple attackers. No matter the threat, my students will survive, walk away, and live to see tomorrow.

I still wanted to do more. In addition to TIG Tactical, I started *Stop Sudden Violence*, a nonprofit charity where I offer free self-defense training to recent survivors of physical violence or human trafficking and school teachers or employees. I want to do as much as possible to allow others to live without fear. With all that I've lived and the training I received, my goal is to teach everyday people to protect themselves from everyday threats.

Hunter Allen, Founder and President
TIG Tactical
www.tigtactical.com

BORDER SECURITY: CHAOS KILLS

By Rodney Scott

What is happening along our international borders today is not just about illegal immigration or drug smuggling. It's about border security. Border security *is* national security. The transnational criminal organizations we commonly call cartels are the ones with complete control of our southwest border, *not* the U.S. government. Instead of us, these cartels are deciding, minute by minute, who and what gets to enter our home.

The open borders created by the previous presidential administration's policies were a national security threat at multiple levels. With specific regard to the travesty of human trafficking, *border security matters*. Today, more than at any other time in my three-decade-long career, we have a preventable humanitarian disaster that—without any doubt—is spoon-feeding vulnerable individuals directly into the human trafficking trade. It is very important to understand that, to a great extent, the cartels also control who the U.S. Border Patrol actually apprehends – and who they do not!

Allow me to explain. Right now, as you read these words, cartel underlings are controlling each and every illegal crossing along the U.S. border with Mexico. Cartels have paid informants, lookouts, and even corrupt officials on both sides of the border. These informants have *already* provided highly accurate information about the real-time law enforcement resources deployed along the southern border and on the highways leading into the U.S. away from the border. The cartel boss has decided and given orders to subordinates about when, where, and how many illegal aliens (even down to the specific nationalities and demographics) to push across the border. The sole objective of the cartel boss is to overwhelm law enforcement.

In many smuggling events, cartels actually *prefer* the first group to surrender or get caught. However, if the first group gets away, so be it. They know that rhetoric and policies of "catch and release" have provided the cartel with an endless flow of *humans* to use as shields. Shields that help to obscure their nefarious narcotics, human smuggling, and human trafficking schemes.

Once all the law enforcement in the area is busy dealing with the first wave of illegal aliens, the cartel brings across the second wave with minimal risk of being caught. That second wave includes anyone—and anything—the cartel wants to get into the U.S.

Sometimes, the second wave is observed and even documented by U.S. Border Patrol, but there are no agents left to respond. These illegal entries are documented as known "got-a-ways." In March 2023, the Chief of the U.S. Border Patrol, Raul Ortiz, testified in March that Border Patrol had *already* documented over 385,000 got-a-ways in Fiscal Year 2023. In Fiscal Year 2022, the U.S. Border Patrol reported nearly 600,000 known got-a-ways. My personal experience has taught me that many times, the second wave is effectively hidden from view and goes completely undetected. These are the unknown got-a-ways.

No documentation or evidence of who or what got into our country exists.

At the time of this writing, in Fiscal Year 2023, CBP has played this cat-and-mouse game over 1.3 million times. That equates to well over 6,000 encounters *every 24 hours*—and that number only represents those taken into custody.

It is important to understand how much time it takes to process over 6,000 people from multiple nations speaking multiple different languages. First, agents must transport these individuals back to a station. This is routinely done in twelve-passenger vans or normal patrol vehicles. In the Senate hearing on March 28, 2023, a senator stated that a Border Patrol Sector Chief told him they had recently encountered people from over 176 different nationalities, speaking over 200 different languages and dialects. Border Patrol agents speak English and Spanish. Everything else requires virtual support from contract language services via phone or the internet. That means more time! Additionally, there are only so many computer terminals and telephones in each station. Expansion is often not an option due to bandwidth limitations.

The result is *total chaos*, which is what the cartels and other human traffickers love and exploit.

An ACLU study revealed that 72% of known trafficking victims in the U.S. are immigrants. A review of trafficking prosecutions in 2021 revealed that 49% of adult cases were, in fact, illegal aliens.

When you look at the current border crisis and consider the trafficking of children, it is even more concerning. First and foremost, it is important to know that U.S. Customs and Border Protection does not routinely keep a photo or fingerprints for any alien under the age of fourteen. DNA testing is only conducted when an agent can articulate a suspicion that the child is being trafficked.

Due to the total chaos associated with processing over 6,000 illegal aliens each day, the agents simply do not have time to conduct thorough investigative interviews to develop the articulable suspicion of trafficking or even assess a claimed family relationship with co-travelers in any meaningful way. *Is that really this child's dad?* There is no feasible way to tell for sure. In all but the most egregious events, agents are forced to accept the information being provided at face value.

It is also important to note that many victims of trafficking do not know they are being trafficked when they initially enter the country illegally. They are often still under the belief that the smuggler is just providing a service to get them into the U.S. under the radar. They don't find out the truth until it is too late.

Under prior Administrations, as the border security environment was constantly improving and illegal immigration was slowing down dramatically, agents had more time to conduct in-depth interviews and identify inconsistencies in claimed family members' stories. Agents identified countless cases where a child or adult admitted they were not related. We will never know for sure how many children were rescued before they were able to be victimized further.

Any unaccompanied alien child the U.S. Border Patrol encounters is transferred to the U.S. Department of Health and Human Services (HHS) as quickly as possible. HHS is responsible for placing the child with a "sponsor." Unfortunately, HHS is underfunded, overworked, lacks the ability to continue systematic monitoring after a child is placed with a sponsor, and is hamstrung by politics, preventing any meaningful investigation into sponsors or claimed guardians. The bottom line? *Chaos kills.*

Chaos provides cover for all types of criminal activity. As a direct result of the catch-and-release policies implemented by the Biden administration, our international border with Mexico and our immigration process for unaccompanied alien children have devolved into total chaos. Chaos that is ripe for exploitation by human traffickers.

It does *not* have to be this way. Deterrence policies and programs work. The U.S. Border Patrol has countless examples to show that if you simply enforce the law, hold people accountable, and avoid releasing aliens into the U.S. until after a judge has adjudicated their case, cross-border illegal entries dramatically decrease. This immediately increases the time that agents can investigate and mitigate more sophisticated criminal schemes like narcotics smuggling and human trafficking.

Border security is national security. Border security saves lives.

Rodney Scott served as the 24th Chief of the United States Border Patrol prior to 2021. After thirty years in the Border Patrol, under bipartisan administrations, he is a Senior Distinguished Fellow for Border Security. He provides America's leading state-based think tank with analysis and recommendations on both federal, state and local border security efforts.
www.texaspolicy.com/about/staff/rodney-scott/

OVERCOMING EXPLOITATION: AN OVERVIEW OF EXPRESSIVE ARTS IN RESTORATIVE CARE

By Danielle Freitag, LADC

"If you are involved in addressing victims of sexual abuse, they need movement. They literally need to dance."

- DR. DAN ALLENDER

As the bright South African sun shone down inside the gates of the safe house, it was the perfect day to incorporate dance. Even though the space was small, there was enough room to move as needed. Just as I had done so many times over the years, I was incorporating dance as a form of healing within the series of restorative workshops I was there to conduct. Movement in the form of dance would make a way for healing from the trauma of the not-so-distant past.

Each of the girls stepped rhythmically to the notes that carried a familiar sound. They had become accustomed to some of the music that played at the safe house and the church they attended. There was so much emotion that went into each step, as if the movement was all that mattered.

After a time of free dance, choreography was created for a song about being forgiven. A song called *Speak the Name* by Koryn Hawthorne sounded loudly as the girls stepped in sync with the words.

As the girls danced, their feet moving in strong, rhythmic motion to the sound of freedom. They experienced healing.

Several times before that day, I, too, experienced healing because of dance. It had been a little more than a decade since I had last been in South Africa. The first time, I was one of several individuals from around the world who were accepted into a unique, faith-based arts ministry. The ministry incorporated dance and music in a relevant way through theater to share the gospel message. During that time, whether it was choreographed or freestyle, dance allowed me to reconnect with beauty and innocence.

As a little girl, I loved to sing and dance. I also loved to create. At first, I would twirl and leap around the house like a ballerina, never thinking I needed to have anyone to dance for. Like many young girls, I had taken years of dance lessons—jazz, tap, and ballet. At that time, there was a sense of innocence in the way I moved. No matter what expression, dance has been something I've enjoyed from the beginning.

Dance has also brought healing from the past—a past where movement became seductive and controlled in the commercial sex industry. For about six years, the strip club industry and all that came with it sought to keep me entangled in a world of seduction, addiction, and various forms of abuse.

That day in South Africa, as I danced alongside other girls who had also experienced exploitation, marked fourteen years since I got out of the industry and into a life of freedom. A lot had changed for me in that time. My journey of restoration wouldn't have been possible without practicing sobriety, as well as the other therapeutic tools that I learned and put into practice.

Now, as a Licensed Alcohol and Drug Counselor, advocate for women, and fellow overcomer healing from trauma, I have the honor and privilege of teaching the same tools that I learned to the incredible women I get to meet.

Evidence-Based Practices

Women who've experienced exploitation or any form of sexual abuse can often struggle with mental illness and substance use disorders (SUD) in complex ways. Trauma and SUD are often concurrent conditions. If addressing trauma, problematic substance use must be addressed, as trauma cannot be effectively treated if someone is turning to substances as a means to cope.

We know that trauma can have a lasting effect on a person's well-being. The good news is the healing that comes from new experiences and tools practiced to promote well-being can also be lasting. Restoration is absolutely possible, and best therapeutic practices will help.

The best therapeutic practices are person-centered, holistic, and foster self-efficacy to empower choices that are reflective of one's values. One example is Expressive Arts Therapy. The goal for anyone who has experienced trauma from exploitation is restoration—body, spirit, and soul. Before diving into the relevance of dance as a form of healing, allow me to share the best therapeutic practices for working with female overcomers of commercial sexual exploitation.

First of all, trauma-informed care is a *strengths-based* approach "that is grounded in an understanding of and responsiveness to the impact of trauma; that emphasizes physical, psychological, and emotional safety for both providers and survivors; that creates opportunities for survivors to rebuild a sense of control and empowerment."[12]

Three of the six core principles of trauma-informed care (TIC), according to SAMHSA (Substance Abuse and Mental Health Services Administration), include:

- **Safety**: Policy and practice reflect a commitment to provide physical and emotional safety for service recipients and staff.
- **Choice & Empowerment**: To facilitate healing and avoid retraumatization, choice and empowerment are part of trauma-informed service delivery for both service recipients and staff.
- **Strengths-Based**: With a focus on strength and resilience, service recipients and staff build skills that will help them move in a positive direction.[13]

Empowerment is essential to healing. Because of this, self-efficacy is a concept that must be understood by anyone providing direct services. Self-efficacy is the belief in one's capabilities to achieve a goal or an outcome. For an outcome to be healthy, an individual must be aligned with thoughts and actions that truly promote wellness. In contrast, internal conflict is the outcome of actions opposite of what a person values and opposite of the thoughts and/or actions that produce wellness. When someone

---

[12] Elizabeth K. Hopper, Ellen L. Bassuk, and Jeffrey Olivet, "Shelter from the Storm: Trauma-Informed Care in Homeless Service Settings," *The Open Health Services and Policy Journal* 3 (2010): 80-100.

[13] *SAMHSA's Concept of Trauma and Guidance for a Trauma-Informed Approach* (2014): 10. Pub ID#: SMA14-4884.

is focused on healthy coping skills, the chances of disengaging from unhealthy coping skills increase.

Assisting one who has experienced the violation of the body and soul means leading that person, by means of empowerment, toward healthy coping skills. Most importantly, it means being connected to the One who can heal all wounds and offer the best leadership and the needed ability to make change, Jesus Christ.

When someone is feeling empowered, it means they feel enabled and motivated toward greater responsibility and authority in their own life to make healthy, and oftentimes better, choices. While this description of empowerment is true, there is more to be understood about the word empowerment, which is often used in the anti-trafficking movement.

Within the therapeutic skill and evidence-based practice of motivational interviewing, the power of choice, or self-efficacy, is promoted. When someone better understands the choices available and what those choices could mean, empowerment is present. But where does this new strength to carry out better choices come from? To understand, we must look at the root meaning of the word empowerment.

The Greek verb, **Endunamoó** (*en-doo-nam-ó-o*) means to empower. The Greek verb ***dunamoó*** means "To make strong and enable."[14] The strength spoken of in the word *endunamoó* is not self-made, but is strength given or shared. The short definition of the word *endunamoó* means, "I fill with power, strengthen, make strong." Notice the definition alludes to the truth that there is power coming from someone else.

---

14   *NAS Exhaustive Concordance of the Bible with Hebrew-Aramaic and Greek Dictionaries* (The Lockman Foundation, 1998).

Jesus is the "I" that supplies empowerment. We know this because, in Matthew 28:18 (NIV), we are told by Jesus Himself, "*All power is given unto me in heaven and on earth.*" The woman who sought desperately to get to Jesus had faith that just touching the hem of His robe would bring healing to her.

> Just then, a woman who had been subject to bleeding for twelve years came up behind him and touched the edge of his cloak. She said to herself, "If I only touch his cloak, I will be healed." Jesus turned and saw her. "Take heart, daughter," he said, "your faith has healed you." And the woman was healed at that moment.
> **(MATTHEW 9:20-22 NIV)**[15]

Truth be told, I've related to this woman in profound ways through the years. Often, I've had to push past the influence of the culture and other voices just to hear Him and experience what only He can provide, which is Himself.

It is in His power, and only from this place of strength, that life can be truly empowered and transformed. For any overcomer of trauma or addiction, His power through the Holy Spirit can bring change, for it is "*Christ who dwells in our hearts through faith*" (Ephesians 3:17 NIV). That power is available to provide the capacity that is needed to make ongoing, wise, and healthy choices.

In addition to best therapeutic practices like CBT (Cognitive Behavioral Therapy), motivational interviewing, and implementing individual behavioral interventions, music, dance, and art are absolutely necessary for true freedom and healing.

---

15 *Holy Bible, New International Version*® (Biblica, Inc.™, 2011).

Dance as Therapy

Because of the body memory associated with seductive and exploitative movements, it was pivotal for me, just as it is for any woman coming out of sexual trauma or exploitation, to learn to move in a different way. An aspect of my own healing occurred because I was able to reconnect my body to innocence through dance; through movement.

> "If you are involved in addressing victims of sexual abuse, they need movement. They literally need to dance. They literally need to have their bodies return to them by an acknowledgment of the fact that we are sinews, muscles. We are bones and movement. What evil wishes to do through the experience of betrayal is to turn you against your body and, through powerlessness, to take away your effectiveness in this world and ultimately to bring shame to your body."
> **- DR. DAN ALLENDER**[16]

The first mention of movement in scripture ushers in the very act of creation by the Creator. It is the Holy Spirit's movement followed by God's spoken word that ushers in the following days of creation: *"And the Spirit of God was hovering over the waters"* (Genesis 1:2 NIV). "Hovering" is the Hebrew word *Rachaph*, which means to hover, flutter, or move. It was movement that ushered in change.

The first mention of dance in scripture occurs as a response to leaving slavery. Miriam and the Israelites see the great power of God, who delivers them from their enemy. After the parting of the Red Sea, Miriam expresses her emotion through dance:

---

[16] Dan Allender, "Abolition Summit - Enduring Through Brokenness," presented at the Exodus Cry 2013 Summit, 2013.

"*Then Miriam the prophetess, the sister of Aaron, took a tambourine in her hand, and all the women went out after her with tambourines and dancing*" (Exodus 15:20 NIV).

It was movement that Miriam engaged in as a celebration of coming out of oppressive conditions. She felt so much joy in seeing the miracle that she simply had to dance. The harsh conditions of slavery would be experienced no more.

Art as Therapy

In addition to appropriate dance being an effective way to heal, creating through the arts is considered an evidence-based practice.

Anna Friendt, Founder of Anna Friendt Artwork and Illustration, is passionate about creatively pointing hearts toward healing and restoration. Anna, who is also a wife, mother, and survivor of exploitation, tells us:

> "Creativity never begins with the act of creating. It begins with a thought or idea, often derived from or motivated by a story. Creativity brings new life into situations that feel dead. It is the ingredient required for bringing change to the world. Art speaks into and about our lives in ways that words cannot. We all are called to create. We are all able to participate. To make, mold, or assemble. To speak, sing, dance, or write, to create a change. To compose in a way that impacts our world. When hearts encounter healing, our communities are built up and restoration follows suit. It is a process that works from the inside and moves outward, causing a ripple effect."

For Anna, art became a tool in her life, which led to hope. She found healing through creating art, which helped her overcome the after-effects and trauma from abuse, rejection, and exploitation. She knows that the creative process can reveal so much about the condition of the heart: wounds to be healed, dreams to be ignited, and needs to be fulfilled. What I have come to find in working with clients over the last decade is that those who engage in creating art better understand their thoughts, emotions, and experiences.

Music as Therapy

This chapter would not be complete without addressing the power of music. I attribute a great deal of my own healing not only to listening to worship music, but playing worship music on the piano and spending time singing.

From my second book, *The Garden Keys V.II, Awakening Daughter Zion*:

> "Science has been hard at work trying to explain why singing has such a calming, yet energizing, effect on people. What researchers are beginning to discover is that singing is like an infusion of the perfect tranquilizer, the kind that both soothes your nerves and elevates the happy chemicals in your brain. The surge of calm that comes from singing comes from endorphins, a hormone which is associated with feelings of pleasure."[17]

The amygdala, an almond-shaped mass of cells located deep within the temporal lobes of your brain, is a part of the limbic system structure that is involved in your emotions and motivations, particularly those that are related to survival. The processing of emotions such as fear, anger, and pleasure are all a part of

---

17   Danielle Freitag, *The Garden Keys - 22 Keys of Restoration: V.II - Awakening Daughter Zion* (Footprint Publishing, 2019).

the amygdala. The amygdala is also responsible for determining which memories are stored and where they are kept in the brain. It is thought that this determination is based on the size of the emotional response an event evokes.

Describing the relationship between trauma, singing, and the amygdala, Dr. Dan Allender states:

> "We need to understand that when you've been traumatized, your brain changes. A portion of your limbic system called the hippocampus shrinks somewhere up to 8-12 percent, and that part of our brain regulates emotions. There is a portion of your brain affected by trauma called the amygdala. It's an interplay between the amygdala and the hippocampus. The hippocampus shrinks as a result of trauma, but can grow to the degree we begin to tell our stories in a way in which we can regulate our own body's struggle. When you sing and hear music, your amygdala dances. Your brain changes when you sing, when you hear music, when you worship, when you have a chance to be in the presence of beauty. Your body begins to change."[18]

Pleasure hormones like endorphins and oxytocin are released during singing. These hormones have been found to alleviate anxiety and stress. Oxytocin also enhances feelings of trust and bonding, which may explain why many studies have found that singing lessons decrease feelings of depression and loneliness.

Singing can literally help move us from fear to freedom, from sadness to happiness. Taking this a step further, singing the Word of God gets the truth into the soul (mind, emotions, and will). There is a hunger in the human heart to create, whether

---

18 Dan Allender, "Abolition Summit - Enduring Through Brokenness," presented at the Exodus Cry 2013 Summit, 2013.

it be through song, dance, or the arts. We were made to create like our Creator.

Call to Action

Allow me to propose the following solutions for anyone working directly with survivors of sexual abuse, including sexual exploitation, which is a human rights violation:
- Include healthy, appropriate dance as an aspect of best-care practices
- Include Expressive Arts Therapy
- Support organizations offering the above as therapeutic services. There is a need for trauma care that incorporates these practices
- Ensure that anyone working directly with survivors of exploitation has proper training to understand complex trauma

Now, just like the girls in South Africa, I dance to express freedom as a restored, healed woman who dances not for an audience or a man in movements of seduction. I no longer move like the puppet who was held by strings of entanglement that influenced me to bring arousal while club managers profited off of exploiting me.

Now there is innocence, beauty, and liveliness in movements that usher in connection with my Creator—the One who created me body, spirit, and soul.

Our daughters are treasures, not commodities.

Danielle Freitag, LADC
Author, Executive Director - Action 169
action169.com

TURNING A MILLION EYES TO SAVE LIVES

By Deborah S. Sigmund

During the summer of 2003 in the South of France, I first heard the term "human trafficking." I was with a woman from Switzerland who helped victims who were forced into the underground world of the sex trade. As a mother, I was horrified that this was happening in the world today and that it was a huge business. When I returned home to Washington, D.C., I hugged my thirteen-year-old a little longer and tighter and promised that this would never happen to her. I realized something had to be done to make people aware of this monstrous crime, and I was determined to help protect children everywhere.

Back in Washington, I began talking about what I had learned about child trafficking everywhere I went. Through a friend, I met the Under Secretary of State Paula Dobriansky, who invited me to the State Department to meet her team in the Trafficking in Persons Office. During the meeting, I was told, "We need you to help us raise awareness about the issue." When I responded that I had a group of friends who all cared deeply about the issue, Under Secretary Paula Dobriansky suggested we start a nonprofit. After a series of meetings, Innocents at Risk was established in 2005.

One of Innocents at Risk's first projects was to create an awareness film.

The film was being produced by Director Carl Colby, who suggested we interview well-known people of authority for the film. Having learned about the mission of Innocents at Risk through The Embassy of Sweden, Her Majesty Queen Silvia invited me to the Royal Palace in Stockholm to meet with her. From that meeting, she agreed to be interviewed for the awareness film as she had been a powerful voice in the fight against human trafficking since 2001.

Along with Her Majesty Queen Silvia, the film featured interviews with the Under Secretary of State Paula Dobriansky, Congressman Christopher Smith, a diplomat from the Embassy of Nigeria, the entertainer Ricky Martin, and a survivor of trafficking. The film made its first debut in 2007 at the *Innocents at Risk Gala*. This film became a powerful awareness tool to be used with embassies in Washington, D.C. churches, schools, and organizations across the United States and around the world.

In 2008, the Ambassador of Colombia, Carolina Barco, agreed to host a dinner for Innocents at Risk at her residence. Learning about this event, a senior flight attendant from American Airlines, Sandra Fiorini, informed me that flight attendants were seeing what we were talking about—but they didn't know what to do about it. Realizing that this was a tremendous opportunity to save lives, Innocents at Risk decided to produce a training brochure to inform flight attendants about signs of human trafficking in airports and on planes.

Innocents at Risk worked with The Department of State and the Polaris Project (National Human Trafficking Hotline) to produce a training brochure called *Protecting Women and Children from Human Trafficking*. Under the leadership of Sandra Fiorini and with thousands of brochures, flight attendants began training one another. This initiative expanded to airlines such as American Airlines, Delta, United, Southwest, and U.S. Air. Within the first year, we trained approximately 1,000 flight attendants with the National Human Trafficking Hotline.

Realizing this was a powerful force, Innocents at Risk introduced the Department of Homeland Security (DHS) to the Flight Attendant Initiative in 2009. After DHS learned about the importance of what the flight attendants were seeing on the planes, they announced that this was a great breakthrough! Thereafter, DHS referred to Innocents at Risk as their "boots in the air." After several meetings, we established a more efficient protocol called Blue Lightning. This protocol is still used today.

Later that year, I introduced the Flight Attendant Initiative (Blue Lightning) to Nancy Rivard of Airline Ambassadors. Airline Ambassadors continues to work with Innocents at Risk to train flight attendants and airline personnel in the United States and abroad. Congressman Chris Smith organized a Congressional Briefing in 2010 for Innocents at Risk and Airline Ambassadors to inform American Airlines, Delta, United, Southwest, and U.S. Air about our work with flight attendants.

From that briefing, American Airlines began training their flight attendants with information from the "Protecting Women and Children from Human Trafficking" brochure. They also referenced the Innocents at Risk website in their annual training manual. At that point, the Secretary of Transportation Raymond LaHood requested a meeting with Innocents at Risk, where he agreed to get everyone in transportation trained. This began the partnership between Innocents at Risk, DHS, DOT, and organizations such as Truckers Against Trafficking.

As countless stories from flight attendants, airline personnel, and experienced travelers came to our attention, we realized human trafficking was happening everywhere; it was difficult to solely rely on the flight attendants and airline personnel to catch every situation. In talking with the Department of Homeland Security/Blue Lightning, Innocents at Risk decided it was time to get the general public involved. We wanted to educate everyone on what to look out for in airports, on planes, train stations, bus terminals, or wherever you may be, as human trafficking is happening all around us.

In 2021, Innocents at Risk established a podcast, *Turning a Million Eyes to Save Lives*, to mobilize the general public. This podcast is an educational tool that informs listeners about the grave issue of human trafficking and teaches everyday citizens how to recognize and report red-flag situations of suspected human trafficking. Through conversations with flight attendants, officers with the Department of Homeland Security, the National Center for Missing and Exploited Children, non-profit organizations, government transportation officials, and teachers, the general public gains a better understanding of human trafficking and what is being done to stop it. The more people that are aware of this situation, the more eyes we will have on the ground.

This message is a reminder that you don't have to be a flight attendant to report a situation and save a life. **Today is a call to action.** If you see something on the streets, in a mall, at a bus stop, train station, airport or anywhere else, if you see something suspicious that doesn't look right, *please report suspected human trafficking* to the DHS at 1-866-347-2423.

You could be saving a life.

Deborah S. Sigmund, Founder
Innocents at Risk

Editor's Note: This was the last article written from Charter Voices Against Trafficking™ Member, Deborah Sigmund, who sadly passed away on January 4, 2023. Her words remain in our hearts, and her lifetime of advocacy for the innocents leaves a legacy for generations to come.

COURAGE IS CONTAGIOUS:
THE TRUE STORY OF CRYSTAL CHEN'S
FIGHT FOR HUMAN RIGHTS

By Andi Buerger, JD

Growing up, Crystal Chen had no idea that her life would ever be in imminent danger. She also never imagined that one unexpected miracle would turn her voice into a champion for millions of others whose voices have been summarily silenced by a powerful world government.

Raised in Guangzhou City, a sprawling port city northwest of Hong Kong on the Pearl River in China, Crystal lived with her parents and an older brother. Her mother and father were loving and generous, working hard to help mold their daughter's character. Her father worked for the Guangzhou Performing Arts Company, where he played the traditional Chinese musical instrument er-hu, or what would be known today as a two-string violin. Her mother was an acclaimed soprano singer. Though highly accomplished in the arts, her parents were genuine, kind, and helpful to others around them.

As a result of the artistic influence in her family, Crystal developed talents in dancing, singing, and theatrical performance at a very young age. She was invited to be part of a Chinese television series as well as a few movies in her teen years. As exciting and memorable as these opportunities were, her education was also important to her.

Crystal finished elementary school and went on to high school in Guangzhou, where she grew up. Her high school, however, was not like the other high schools in China. Hers was an old missionary boarding school with more than one hundred years of history, whose mission was: Believe. Hope. Love. The Chinese government eventually "normalized" this historical educational site to suit its socio-political belief system. Crystal says, "I think it's because of this very special high school that it gave me a good moral and spiritual background." This was a rare experience in China because it was, and still is, a communist country.

After high school, she attended college in a northern province (similar to a U.S. state) called Anhui. After four years, Crystal earned her Bachelor's Degree in economics. From there, she was hired as a corporate executive for one of the nation's largest import and export corporations.

In 1992, a practice known as Falun Dafa was introduced to the Chinese public. A spiritual discipline, it is also commonly known as *Falun Gong*. Falun Gong consists of moral teachings and five gentle exercises that offer effective and rewarding ways to improve a person's health and energy level. Many people in China, including Crystal, were attracted to Falun Gong's teachings for self-improvement, which are based on its three principles of practice: truthfulness, compassion, and tolerance.

As Falun Gong grew in popularity, practice sessions began showing up all over China, including in public parks. Crystal began practicing Falun Gong in 1997, at the height of its popularity. Soon after, her mother became paralyzed from a serious stroke. Her mother was also diagnosed with late-stage breast cancer while in the ICU.

When her mother had gained enough strength, Crystal had the opportunity to practice Falun Gong with her. It turned out that this practice would cause the miraculous—and documented—transformation in her mother's health as a result of the practices that had made Falun Gong so attractive to millions of Chinese people. "I feel that I have found a deeper, more rewarding path in Falun Gong. It has changed everything for me because I was born and raised in Communist China. Even at birth, I was still brainwashed. I was told that religion was a poison. There should be no religious belief. There was no God. No Buddha. No higher being. Nothing. That is why Falun Gong changed my life."

Although her father did not practice Falun Gong, he did benefit from the changes in his family resulting from the practice of his wife and daughter. The healing Crystal's mother experienced from life-threatening health issues, and more positive attitudes within the home created a pleasant environment for the Chen family. "Even though we had been very close from the start," she recounts, "Falun Gong made it better." So much so that she has been practicing this spiritual discipline for over 26 years. As for her brother, while he may not be a Falun Gong practitioner, he is a "good boy," according to his little sister.

In the beginning, the Chinese government and its state media endorsed Falun Gong for its moral teaching and *proven* health benefits. According to the government's own estimate, in 1999, there were 70-100 million people practicing Falun Gong. However, in July 1999, the Chinese Communist Party (CCP) launched a massive and violent campaign to eradicate Falun

Gong. Why would the government now suppress a practice that they had previously endorsed?

That year, the CCP completely turned every Falun Gong practitioner's life upside down. Crystal remembers that in April 1999, the government started to say negative things about Falun Gong, but "no one knew why." Since the state media controlled everything that people learned through television or radio, a number of Falun Gong practitioners petitioned to speak directly to government officials. They wanted to talk about the truth of what Falun Gong practiced to the people in charge since the state media was promoting slander and rumors. In July 1999, the CCP banned the practice of Falun Gong. In just two short years, Falun Gong fell from government endorsement as a positive practice to a forbidden choice, even worthy of persecution.

The popularity and independence of Falun Gong was perceived as a threat to the Chinese Communist Party. After all, the Party membership was about 70 million people, while the Falun Gong population was reported at 100 million. Falun Gong's principles contrast those of the CCP. The nature of the Chinese Communist Party is all about lies, deceit, and killing, according to Crystal. If people make their own choices, then the CCP cannot control them. The CCP is fearful that someone or something bigger than their regime exists. Falun Gong practitioners believe in a higher being. "We are spiritual," she explains. "Spiritual belief is not about control. It is about improving oneself."

With so many millions of active Falun Gong practitioners, the CCP chose to demonize and politicize the ancient spiritual practice to the world at large in order to justify the persecution of practitioners and unrelenting human rights abuses. Labeled as a *cult*, the government wanted Falun Gong to be seen as "very dangerous" to Westerners. But Falun Gong was never an orga-

p, nor has it ever had a membership. The practitioners ow how many people practice the ancient discipline, only that it is freely offered to all people.

Crystal remembers in 1998, the year after she started to practice Falun Gong, that her workplace suddenly had to give every employee who practiced Falun Gong a "health survey" to learn about the before-and-after results and benefits of that discipline. The Chinese government announced the results, which showed that approximately 97% of the people surveyed said there were definite health benefits. But in the 1990s, every company in China was state-owned. There were no private companies. The employees did not realize the government was actually using the survey to collect information about Falun Gong practitioners: "We were innocent. We didn't realize that the survey had all the numbers of the Falun Gong population. Now, the government knew *who* the practitioners were, where they lived, and all of their personal information."

Soon after the ban was announced in July of 1999, the survey results were announced. Crystal's boss approached her at work and said, "Give up Falun Gong, or you're going to lose your job." She told her boss that she did not want to give up her belief because it was good for her. Her boss replied, "Well, it's not your personal practice anymore. It's banned by the government." She was demoted to a factory worker three hours away from home in a remote area for several months in order for her to "think about" her choice. Crystal refused to give up her belief and subsequently lost her job.

Believing that her story of how Falun Gong had benefited her and her family might change some minds, Crystal headed off to the state, city, and local government. She questioned why they would shut down such a beneficial practice and meditation.

She asked officials how they could force her to denounce Falun Gong and call it a lie. How could the government call it a cult? In her words, "I was very naive."

The persecution of Falun Gong practitioners started in 1999 and is still going on. From 1999 to 2004, Crystal was arrested multiple times. She was put into detention centers, brainwashing centers (to get her to denounce her practice), and forced labor camps. The Chinese government held no legal trials for Falun Gong practitioners. The only options for those unwilling to give up their belief were incarceration or torture, oftentimes both.

According to Crystal, "Forced labor is a major thing for the Communists to use to suppress a 'prisoner of conscience'. "Both my mom and I were put in jail. We were forced to work in appalling conditions sixteen hours a day. We had to make anything from hand-embroidered tops to jeans, shoes, artificial flowers, Christmas lights, and even stuffed animals. That is why in the U.S., I do not buy those things. I was shocked to find out that some of the things we made had the Disney label on it." Laborers like Crystal suffered horrible beatings, deprivation of food, sexual harassment, and handcuff scratching and hanging, which is a specific torture technique.

Her first detention locally in December 1999 lasted fifteen days. One of the first and worst torture techniques was called "forced feeding." CCP police guards and several male prisoners would pin Crystal to the concrete floor and force-feed her with one pound of an all-salt mixture. Because of the mixture, which could have killed her, she choked and lost consciousness. "I felt I was going to die. I felt there was nothing I could do but turn to my belief. I basically prayed to be saved." Moments later, one of the four male prisoners suddenly fainted on the floor. It interrupted the torture process because they needed to have four males. "I realized that it was a miracle to me. *Because I prayed.*"

Crystal continued, "I feel very grateful that God is watching me and that a higher being is watching me. I prayed to be saved. That's the first thing I realized was that prayer *is* powerful." For several days, Crystal was not able to speak or eat due to the effects of the forced salt feeding. However, a male Falun Gong practitioner was not so lucky. He died after being tortured the same way.

Despite the horrific experience of her first detention, Crystal did not give up on her quest to bring the truth about Falun Gong to officials. She went to Beijing, the central government of China, and was placed in a detention center in a northern province. Since the detention center was full, the Chinese Communist Party police guards handcuffed her to a radiator pipe in the police department office with her toes barely touching the ground.

She was left there for three days. A police chief groped Crystal's body while she hung from the pipe. She had no way to protect herself. As the police chief groped her body, she saw his badge. She immediately shouted out his badge number. "I think that God just gave me wisdom to remember that number. I shouted, 'I remember your I.D. When I get out, I will bring you to justice.' He was shocked when I said that. I just kept yelling and shouting out the truth of Falun Gong." Finally, the police chief stopped.

At yet another detention center, the guards threatened Crystal that because she was so stubborn, she would be sent to a mental institution where she would be raped. While she was very thankful to be spared that horror, other women were not. She saw many who were horribly tortured because they would not give up their beliefs in Falun Gong. According to Crystal,

"I survived because of my strong spiritual beliefs. There was a higher power protecting me at critical moments."

Desperation and heartache continued to follow her as both she *and* her mother were put in jail. The CCP guards purposely separated the mother and daughter, and it would be years before the two women would finally see or speak to each other. In the labor camp, Crystal's mother endured unconscionable torture. She was once shocked with electric batons for almost two hours before she fainted. CCP guards poured water on her to make the shock more intense. Crystal's mother was eventually released due to physical health issues, but not long after, she passed away. Her mother died *not* because of failing health but because of the *Chinese government*. The unrelenting torture destroyed the body that the practice of Falun Gong had once fully healed from a life-threatening illness.

During her years in forced labor camps, health exams were given to test the blood of Falun Gong practitioners—but *only* those prisoners. Allegations that Falun Gong practitioners were being killed to harvest their organs were first disclosed to the international community in 2006. The blood tests were necessary to check blood type compatibility between the organs harvested and the organ recipients. Organ harvesting of Falun Gong practitioners is very different from the black market generally associated with that term. In China, it is a systematic industry with the full collaboration of state hospitals, police, judicial officials, the military, and other agencies. Crystal narrowly escaped becoming one of those involuntary organ donors.

In 2004, she was temporarily released by the labor camp due to a life-threatening physical condition directly resulting from the torture tactics that had been forced upon her. Crystal's heart had a huge problem, even though she was just in her early thirties at the time. The CCP was concerned that she would die in the camp. "They thought that if I died at home, there would be no liability. If I lived, then they would bring me back to the labor camp—and continue to torture me." During her brief release, she managed to escape. In 2005, she was accepted by the United Nations High Commissioner for Refugees (UNHCR).

Currently, Crystal lives in Texas with her husband. She works for The Epoch Media Group as its Director of Partnerships. She believes that working in the media is the best way to get the word out about so many human rights issues. "I am so very grateful to the people who helped me settle in America. Despite the human rights abuse, there *is* still goodness and love in the world."

When asked why she wants the world to know her story, Crystal says, "It is so important to tell the truth. I believe that *courage is contagious.* I walk in freedom. Free of torture. Free of persecution. Free to practice Falun Gong. I can't just leave thousands of other practitioners. I feel I *must* give voice to those that have none, including my mother."

As for her earlier life in China, Crystal wants "everyone to know the evil of the Chinese Communist Party. I want to tell the truth that Falun Gong is *not* a cult. Westerners need to take a fresh look at it and not judge it wrongly." In addition, she hopes to expose the slave labor, organ harvesting, and merciless persecution of Falun Gong practitioners. The persecution once solely focused on practitioners like Crystal has now expanded to other belief-based groups in China, such as the Uyghur, Tibetan Buddhists, and underground Christians in China.

Today, a beautiful and eloquent speaker and advocate for others who have been persecuted, Crystal exudes peace and contentment in her new homeland. "I'm actually happy. I'm very, very happy."

Andi Buerger, JD is Founder of Voices Against Trafficking™. Her books *Voices Against Trafficking™ - The Strength of Many Voices Speaking As One* and *A Fragile Thread of Hope: One Survivor's Quest to Rescue* are available on Amazon.com. Her *Voices of Courage* magazine is available online at *Voices of Courage.media* with a television program, also titled *Voices of Courage*, due out in 2026. Andi's work continues to appear in numerous publications, books, online news outlets, and bestselling titles including *Everyday Triumph - Extraordinary Stories of Hope, Resilience, and Impact*, by Chris Meek, Ed.D.

THE RIPPLES
By Jeff Wagner

I like to encourage people by telling them to "remember the ripples." Remember the positive effects your actions can have without you ever knowing. Of course, the truth is that there are also ripples resulting from the events in our lives that escape all of us. I have rarely shared what I am setting out to share with you today, and in doing so, I can't help but feel as vulnerable as I was when I was a boy of nine.

The year was 1976, and my parents had just built a house outside of the town I grew up in. This move would forever change my life. I was the youngest of four boys and sought to find my own separate identity. My father was a wonderful man, but was also a slave to alcohol and, therefore, absent in many ways. Although I sought to win his approval daily, more often than not, I didn't receive it. My mother had not dealt with being a victim herself. She loved her children but didn't make her dislike of men a secret—she openly reminded all of us regularly. Our lives weren't perfect, but I still loved them and understood they were doing what they could for us.

Feminism was practically militant in the 1970's. I remember some female teachers who were openly hostile to me and all the boys in her classroom, continuously compounding the problems of a confused young boy just trying to be proud of who and what he was. When I hear the phrase "toxic masculinity," I have the same reaction today. These words are peddled by the bitter people who cannot come to terms with their own ripples and, therefore, live in perpetual victimhood.

With this background came the horror of being sexually molested for several years by an older male neighbor. At the time, I didn't even know it was wrong. I didn't see myself as a victim. I knew that as a male, I wasn't supposed to cry, whine, or be weak. I was supposed to make the best of it and not bother others with my problems. Although deeply ashamed, I couldn't bring myself to tell anyone. Instead of ripples, I was in a hot tub with the jets on full power and wouldn't realize it for decades!

The first discovery on the road to recovery for me was realizing I was far from alone in my experience as a male. During this time, I remember all the attention paid to female victims, as if it just didn't happen to males. I saw programs, articles, commercials, classroom, and workplace programs exclusively developed for females. As a sexually molested male, these made me feel isolated and uncared for. I felt unimportant. I wondered why they weren't offered to anyone, including me. What help was there for me?

Over time, more and more men realized the impact of their experiences and came out with their dark secrets. It was liberating. It was finally ok to speak about it. It was *no longer* a sign of weakness to acknowledge it happened. That was the open door that allowed millions of men to finally examine the ripples of abuse in their own lives.

Over the course of many years, I have been able to see myself and my relationships in a new way. I understand my introverted nature. I understand where the lack of confidence and self-respect came from. I understand that by forgiving others, I can forgive myself, allowing me to move on. I understand where my deep need for affection, validation, and recognition from others comes from. I understand why I feel jealous and threatened at times. Through understanding the neverending impact of the ripples of my life, I can now improve. Some surprise me and come along and reinforce the negatives I am left with, making it difficult to be positive. Others reinforce my success in dealing with my past, and I feel wonderful. It's life. I adapt and move on.

I'm proud to have a platform to bring my experiences to others and to use that platform to bring attention to the evil waiting to destroy lives. It is an honor to be a man in the light, doing God's work for good. My advice to those who share similar experiences is to think in terms of the ripples. Make an honest and thorough assessment of your entire being and question why you are *who* you are and what impact the ripples have in your life, both positive and negative.

In the immortal words of Johnny Nash, "I can see clearly now; the rain is gone." After decades that included denial, anger, avoidance, and projection, I can finally say the demon has been slain. The questions I periodically ponder are: Exactly what were the ripples? How did these events change me? Is there anything positive to take away from all this?

The benefits of my experiences? They have taught me to persevere. I am stronger for going through the journey. I am proud that I made it. As a father of three daughters, I raised them with open eyes and protected them to the extent I could without smothering them.

May you find peace within the ripples.

Jeff Wagner is the host of *The Patriot Review* on Frank-Speech.com, RAMtv.live and other streaming and social media platforms. He is also a producer for documentaries. His website is www.redbloodedpatriots.com.

THE "WICKED GOOD" INVESTIGATION

By Eric Caron, U.S. Special Agent
& U.S. Diplomat (Ret.)

On May 12th, 2006, while still working with the Legacy INS National Security Group in Boston, I was asked to review an anonymous tip that came in through our tip line. The tip was related to a business in New Bedford, Massachusetts, identified as Michael Bianco, Inc. (MBI). The caller alleged that the owner of MBI, Francesco Insolia, an Italian immigrant, was knowingly hiring hundreds of illegal aliens and assisting many with obtaining fake or fraudulent identification documents.

The tipster described deplorable working conditions at MBI. These included providing only one roll of toilet paper per stall per day; docking an employee's pay by fifteen minutes for every minute they were late; fining employees twenty dollars for spending more than two minutes in a restroom stall and terminating them for a subsequent offense; fining employees twenty dollars for leaving their work area before the sounding of the bell signaling the break; and fining employees twenty dollars for talking while working and terminating them for additional violations.

What stood out was the fact that the company was a Department of Defense (DOD) contractor that manufactured tactical military vests. It was later discovered that Insolia's wife was the president of a company called Front Line Defense (FLD), which operated out of the same facility. The way MBI did business was to have workers clock in and out on MBI timecards for all hours between 8:00 a.m. and 5:00 p.m. and then clock back in on FLD timecards to avoid overtime compensation.

Based on my training and experience, I noticed several red flags immediately. I harked back to the ESC case, where we had a defense contractor physically offshoring the production of goods and services to Russia. In this case, Insolia simply brought the foreign workers to the U.S. to make the goods. This had broad national security implications. I knew that if terrorists had found their way into the defense contractor's facility, we might be dealing with serious injuries and/or death. I also knew that terrorists could infiltrate and sabotage these goods by, let's say, rubbing a WMD agent like ricin on the vests, potentially resulting in the deaths of our military service members. Some people would say, "No way... that could never happen!"

But it most certainly could, as terrorists are limited only by their imaginations. Utilizing law enforcement technology, I was able to track down the anonymous caller and cultivate her into assisting in the investigation as a Confidential Informant (CI). CIs are the lifeline of any street agent. They are in a position to provide the who, what, when, where, and how of a criminal organization. They can be pivotal in ensuring that we can successfully investigate and prosecute. Confidential Informants could be anyone—from ex-spouses of criminals to competitors who see unfair practices to concerned citizens.

This particular CI was a female, a mother, and the perfect example of a concerned citizen. She was motivated by the desire to do the right thing, but she also had skin in the game because MBI employed her as a stitcher. She was shocked that the owner had so many illegal workers employed and furious that these positions weren't available to the residents of New Bedford. This was a sad state of affairs for New Bedford, which had the highest unemployment rate in the state. MBI had received approximately $57,000 in tax incentives to hire legal citizens. Hundreds and hundreds of legal U.S. citizens could have and should have been employed by MBI with that money. They could have attracted workers not only from Massachusetts but from the neighboring states of New Hampshire, Rhode Island, and New York—people who were willing to relocate to work for a good defense contractor.

MBI could have offered legal U.S. citizens the kind of employment opportunities that would have enabled them to buy groceries, put their kids through school, and buy a home. There is a residual benefit to the economy when you have a corporation hiring legal citizens. I asked myself how this could be happening, with this many alleged illegal aliens in one business. Surely, during DOD visits, they witnessed the deplorable conditions and spoke to workers. So, where was the DOD oversight of this business? Didn't anybody ask the right questions? Didn't anybody from the local, state, or federal government care? As the investigation continued, it became clear that an attitude of willful blindness hovered over the entire city.

The fact that all this was happening in my hometown of New Bedford was hard to swallow. New Bedford had been considered one of the wealthiest cities in America during the whaling days (as depicted in *Moby Dick*). Now, it was one of the worst cities in America. Over several decades, the elected officials of my hometown had failed this once beautiful city. They had poured billions of dollars into the town with little to show for it. They allowed poverty and crime to continue unabated to the point that New Bedford had been, for many years, one of the most crime-ridden cities in the state.

The schools had been labeled as "underperforming" by the state, factories, once bustling had closed, and street crime and opium drug use were the highest in the state. Even the air quality had suffered—as it still does today. (Findings from a May 2017 study done by the University of Iowa and Boston University of Public Health showed that airborne PCB emissions from the New Bedford Harbor constitute the single largest continuous source of airborne PCB ever measured from natural waters in the U.S. and Canada.)

Once a city or corporation gets a reputation for welcoming illegal aliens, word quickly gets out: "As long as you make it to New Bedford, Massachusetts, you'll have a job. No one there really cares about your immigration status." Illegal aliens then start coming in great numbers via whatever means of transport are available—planes, trains, automobiles, etc. That was exactly what happened with MBI. Word got out that they were a safe haven corporation, and illegal alien workers started showing up on their doorstep. And then, thanks to local, state, and federal government officials turning a blind eye, MBI was able to continue to operate.

Globalization is supposed to be such a positive thing for America—but it is like a catnip to transnational criminal groups, enabling them to exploit trade, travel, and telecommunication. Sadly, governments like the U.S. haven't put sufficient measures in place to stop transnational criminals from using globalization to their advantage and to our detriment. This case was right up my alley, and I grabbed onto it like a wild dog with a bone. It was the case I had been waiting for, located in my very own hometown.

When the DOD awards contracts worth hundreds of millions of dollars to one of the largest employers in a depressed city, one would expect the mayor to make a public announcement promoting his city and congratulating MBI. I asked myself, *Why wouldn't the mayor want to show his citizens, his politicians, and others in the state that New Bedford was getting millions in government contracts and putting people to work?* There was no such announcement and no press release. Something didn't add up.

The only reason I could come up with for the mayor's silence was politics. From my perspective, the mayor had to have known that MBI was involved in illegal operations. But no democratic mayor would want to upset the Democratic Party and put themselves in a position where they were denied funding come reelection time. After all, Massachusetts was a Democratic state, and New Bedford was now an unofficial sanctuary city. (The Democratic Party was in support of both illegal aliens and sanctuary cities.) Anything that went against that value system would have upset the Democratic Party. The world of politics can feel like the mafia in the sense that either you're in or you're out. There's no gray area. Even the Catholic Church in New Bedford accepted the influx of illegal aliens.

In 2004, with its membership dwindling, my family's home parish, St. James Church, renamed itself Our Lady of Guadalupe Parish at St. James to appeal to a new Hispanic group of members. Ironically, on May 15th, within days of the anonymous tip coming in concerning MBI, President George W. Bush addressed the nation to discuss "a matter of national importance"—the reform of America's immigration system.

I immediately thought of the anonymous tip and the New Bedford defense contractor allegedly hiring hundreds of illegal aliens to manufacture defense goods for the U.S. military. As President Bush outlined his five goals, he mentioned his support for the temporary work program where foreign workers would be matched with willing American employers for "jobs Americans are not doing." The implication of his statement was clear, and there were subsequent statements that were even clearer. I was shocked. I asked myself, *Did the president just say what I think I heard him say— that Americans are turning down job opportunities because they're lazy?* I wanted to shout at the TV, "Americans would surely do those jobs, Mr. President! You need to fire the advisor who managed to get that line into your speech!" Again, I wondered, *What has happened to my country, my city?*

A couple of months into the development of the MBI case, which I had initiated, I was promoted upstairs to oversee the entire case in a managerial and supervisory capacity. Meanwhile, a senior agent with years of experience and expertise was appointed to work for me as a case agent. After formerly self-demoting to return to the streets, I was now given my grade back. When I was a street agent, I was responsible for my individual cases. As a manager, I was responsible for the entire squad. Now, I had influence over the squad in terms of the direction it was heading, the type of cases we would take on, and who to arrest and prosecute or not. I was in my element, and I found it very fulfilling. I was now the supervisor of all the National Security Division cases at the time, but MBI was my baby. I lived with it on a daily basis.

The newly assigned case agent continued to identify all the illegal aliens while other agents were planning and arranging the introduction into MBI of an undercover case agent (UCA) posing as an illegal alien. A recording of a bad guy admitting to his crime would prove to be powerful evidence for a jury. The CI was able to provide us with not only the who, what, and where, but she took it to the next level. She went into the office manager's office and said, "Hey, I have a friend who needs a job," thereby setting the stage for our undercover operation. The undercover office division maintained dossiers, or profiles, on all our certified Undercover Special Agents. These dossiers were kept top secret, of course, to protect the UCAs. After all, a UCA is getting a whole new identity from passport to driver's license. (Being a UCA sounds very exciting and glamorous until you take into account the extreme risks they have to take.)

I was sent dossiers of several UCAs, and I spent some time reviewing them and interviewing several candidates. Ultimately, I selected a female Spanish-speaking UCA from Texas. The case agent and I spent hours briefing the UCA on the entire case and provided dossiers on the targets. In addition, the UCA spent time getting to know the CI who "dropped the dime" on the bad guys. On September 7, 2006, nearly a dozen agents and the UCA met in a hotel room in an adjacent city. The tech agent provided a phone that would record and transmit the conversations to listening agents. Before showtime, another agent would double-check to make sure the UCA wasn't in possession of her credentials, badge, or weapon.

The cover team was in position, and the green light was given to the UCA to proceed into MBI. Protecting the UCA was paramount, so the cover team monitored transmission for her every move and listened to the transmission for any word of trouble, the sign that they needed to immediately move in to extract her.

With over 500 people in this building, the majority of whom were illegal and some of whom were criminals, the team had to be on their toes and ready to move. Posing as an illegal alien, the UCA entered MBI and began recorded conversations with Insolia and his managers and coworkers. The UCA provided them with a Mexican I.D. and verbally confirmed that she was a Mexican national, not a U.S. resident or citizen, and in fact, illegally present in the U.S. (a necessary element of the violations).

MBI accepted the UCA as an employee, knowing that she was an illegal alien. Then, they instructed her to obtain fraudulent documents at a business across the street from MBI. An employee of this business was previously arrested and, on July 26, 2004, in New York City, convicted of possession of forged documents. Yet, this same employee was now back at work a year later. He charged the UCA $120 for a counterfeit Social Security card and a counterfeit alien registration card with a fake name. These IDs would be presented and accepted as authentic, even though MBI management not only knew these documents were fake, but were the ones who instructed the UCA to obtain them.

We learned a shocking fact: since 2002, the Social Security Administration (SSA) had been sending correspondence to MBI, informing the company that many of the Social Security numbers that MBI provided to SSA pursuant to annual reporting requirements appeared to be fraudulent or invalid. In February of 2007, MBI submitted 646 W-2 payroll records for the tax year 2006. Of those, the SSA determined that 428—more than 66% of the records submitted!—were deficient in some manner. This was a staggering number.

Days later, after passing the sewing test, the UCA was officially hired at MBI. Prior to starting work one particular day, she spoke to two males who said they were in the United States without papers and had no form of identification. The UCA subsequently learned that an office manager hired both men. Demonstrating knowledge of the illegal aliens working at the company, an MBI manager shared with the UCA the fact that many workers from Honduras and Guatemala had paid $5-6,000 to smugglers to get them to MBI.

At the same time, other agents were systematically planning the overall execution of the arrests and search warrants and setting up the immigration processing center we would use to process the illegal aliens after arresting them. The time had come at last for our raid on MBI. By this time, we had briefed the Secretary of Public Safety (the governor's right-hand man), the mayor, the Massachusetts State Police, and all other government entities that might have been impacted by the raid.

With so many illegal aliens in one building, the element of surprise was key to safely and successfully executing this operation. All out-of-state agents were sequestered about sixty miles away in the metro Boston area, cautioned about limiting communications, and reminded to make sure operational security measures were strictly enforced.

There were many agents in on the operation—we could not afford one slip-up. We didn't want an agent inadvertently leaving the operational plan they were reviewing lying around in their hotel room, where prying eyes could see it, or leaving it in a restaurant or a restroom. And the last thing we needed was for an agent to have one too many at the hotel bar one night and start blabbing to a beautiful stranger, "Hey, I'm a federal agent, and we're about to execute a big raid!"

Just one agent who was switched "off" instead of "on" could have torpedoed our operation before it ever got off the ground. So, we reminded everyone of the old adage, "Loose lips sink ships!" Before dawn on March 6, 2007, the morning of the operation, I visited the gravesites of my parents and my brother Eddie, who are buried together. It was a windy, bone-chilling day, with a seven-degree temperature and wind gusts making it even colder. As I said a prayer and mentioned the impending raid, I envisioned Eddie smiling and asking, "Can I come... please?" I envisioned my father telling me how proud he was of my service to our country. And I could almost hear my mom saying, "Be safe!" I thanked them for inspiring me, lifting me up when I was down, and helping me carry the burden of life on the hard days.

I left the cemetery and went directly to the NBPD to brief officers who would be assisting in the raid. It was another "pinch yourself" moment. This was the same police department where my dad worked for nearly eighteen years before his sudden death. As I stood before them, I encouraged safety and professionalism and mentioned that this raid would be closely monitored by the Department of Homeland Security and would probably get news coverage.

Little did I know that this case would be on the front page of most papers in the U.S., including *The Washington Post* and *The New York Times*, and get the attention of the White House, specifically the President. I left the police department and rendezvoused with the seventy-five-car motorcade to initiate and coordinate the multi-site search and arrest operation. As we were getting ready to roll, I needed to make sure all agents were set. The motorcade was ready, and every agent knew their assignment. The surveillance team at MBI was in place and reporting that the target location was clear and ready for us.

The arrest team at the owner's home was in place and ready to take him down. And agents at the document vendor's place of business were ready. Meanwhile, we had a Coast Guard helicopter as our eyes in the sky, an NBPD tactical team standing by, and an NBPD water vessel in the water, ready to rescue any illegal aliens who tried to flee over the hurricane barriers that protected the city against flooding.

Trusting in God—and Our Preparations

We were ready to execute. It was just after 8:00 a.m. I was in the lead vehicle in the front right seat, coordinating with our command post as we made the thirty-minute ride. While we traveled, I received communication that the owner was arrested without incident as he left his home. So far, so good. We were traveling about a twenty-five-mile route from the rendezvous location to the target location. With that many cars, we needed an escort to make sure our motorcade was tight and would arrive intact and safely. Massachusetts State Police and NBPD officers escorted us and did an excellent job of blocking onramps and offramps as we proceeded down to the target location.

We had uniformed police with us in the motorcade and a command center bus, as well—mostly undercover covert vehicles. Of course, the police escort was a dead giveaway. We also had our blue lights ("wig wags") flashing on our grilles. The newspaper later quoted people watching us roll by as saying things like: "I wondered what the hell was going on," and, "I asked myself, 'Are they looking for Osama bin Laden? Are we at war? Or what in the world is happening to have this many police vehicles rolling by at once?"

Quite frankly, our show of force was not overkill, considering that MBI employed about 500 illegal aliens, some of whom were convicted criminals. We couldn't predict what might happen once we got inside the facility or what the reaction to our presence might be.

Desperate people do desperate things. Traditionally and historically speaking, illegal aliens tend to be runners who do not obey law enforcement officers and are prepared to fight if necessary. They tend to be people who are desperate to stay in America and are willing to do—and risk—whatever it takes to escape capture. In the process, they put at risk the lives of law enforcement officers who are simply working to enforce laws enacted by our politicians.

I decided to put the car radio on for just a moment during a lull in the action, and as I did, *Boogie Wonderland* by Earth, Wind & Fire came on. Earth, Wind & Fire was my brother Eddie's favorite band. Hearing them, I felt like he and my father were watching over me. It gave me inspiration and comfort and brought back great memories from my home on Emery Street, only blocks from the target. We were five minutes out from MBI, and the chatter over the radio had come to a halt. There was a palpable solemnity in it.

Everyone knew that with this many illegal aliens at the target location, something was bound to happen. We all knew we were risking our lives to execute this operation, and we didn't know what the outcome was going to be or how many of us would still be standing afterward. We were law enforcement officers, but at that moment, we may as well have been firemen about to enter a burning building. I was also aware from my experience in Washington, D.C., and my time in congressional affairs that this raid had political legs and would resonate, one way or another, with the media. Immigration was such a hot issue. I couldn't possibly have known just how big a media explosion this raid was going to cause. All I could do was say a prayer, have faith in myself and my fellow agents, and believe that everyone was well prepared and practiced in carrying out this type of operation.

We had spent months in planning and preparations. We always trained and prepared extensively because we knew better than to try to make sound decisions with adrenaline coursing through our blood. In times of crisis and chaos, both the body and the mind shut down due to the adrenaline scourge that comes from being in fight-or-flight mode. The mind goes blank unless it has previously been trained to react.

Once you find yourself in a crisis event, it is too late to think of a plan of action. Your only hope is your memory bank. In the heat of battle, the training kicks in at the very moment your conscious mind fails you due to adrenaline rushes and fear. Your mind will automatically retrieve the plan you've rehearsed, assuming that there is a plan in place to retrieve. If you're well-trained, then the body will potentially follow—and both mind and body will be safe. Train enough, and then when "it" hits the fan, you're ready to rock and roll.

We had conducted quarterly drills, varying the conditions. Sometimes we would do drills in daylight and sometimes in the dark. Sometimes we would train inside and sometimes outside. We simulated active shooting situations with paintball guns. If we were doing an indoor drill, we would go into a house and go through the motions of executing warrants and arrests and shoot each other with paintballs.

We would simulate take-cover and concealment techniques. We were trained to instantaneously spot and recognize the kind of objects indoors and out that provide the best cover. When you're indoors, walls and partitions are best—or any barrier made of brick or metal. (Wood and fabric, such as couches and cushions, are not your friends in a gunfire situation.) Outdoors, there are many more options than indoors, including telephone posts, metal garbage dumpsters, and vehicle engine blocks, to name a few.

There is a saying among law enforcement officers: If you fail to prepare, prepare to fail. So, as agents, we were constantly training our minds and bodies for these types of events. We could not afford to freeze and find ourselves unable to function. We had to be fully switched on.

Executing the Wicked Good Raid

We were now sixty seconds from showtime, also known as "Alpha Out" by us agents. One minute later, we were given the go signal from the surveillance vehicle at MBI. The Chief of NBPD had a medical vehicle standing by for us, just in case. My driver was a captain for the Massachusetts State Police. As we approached, he looked at me, shook my hand, and said, "Good luck. Sorry. We can't go in with you." Wait a minute. What? I couldn't believe my ears. I was stunned. It turned out that a week before the raid, word came down that Massachusetts State Police had basically been told by the governor, "Listen, guys... I know you've been helping with the investigation and planning and everything. And you can escort the agents to the location... but don't you dare go into the building and search the premises or arrest any illegal aliens!"

The governor didn't want any of his guys to be seen entering the facility or escorting illegal aliens. It was entirely a political decision made by a Democratic, pro-illegal-alien governor. It would have looked bad for him to be involved in a roundup of illegal aliens. The five hundred souls in the building were approximately half men and half women, including some eighty illegal aliens with previous deportation orders and several with criminal records. These were people who had already gone through the system and been told to leave but didn't. We weren't going after priests and nuns here.

As I entered MBI, I saw the eyes of hundreds and hundreds of third-world-nation people, all slaving away. They looked gaunt and sickly. It didn't look like they had been eating regularly or well. They looked worn down from constantly sitting at tables, slaving away, making U.S. military goods. It was like a scene right out of *The Jungle*, a 1906 novel that portrayed the harsh working conditions and exploited lives of immigrants in the United States. In the movie adaptation, these elements were contrasted with the deeply-rooted corruption of people of power. Little did I know at that moment just how much of a correlation there was between the situation at hand and *The Jungle*. The similarities would prove staggering.

I thought, *What the hell is going on here?* These poor bastards are being abused! We have a sweat-shop environment right here on American soil, and the U.S. Government is doing contracts with them! How in the world does this happen in the building of a U.S. defense contractor? My immediate reaction when I saw the working conditions was, *This can't be real! Not in my country, my state, my city!* But it *was* real, and I was about to stop it.

At my direction, a Spanish-speaking agent announced over the intercom to shut all machines off and not to run. But, of course, within seconds of the announcement, workers began to run. I quickly ordered the rest of my team inside. One pregnant worker collapsed, and one agent fell up the stone stairs, cracking his head open. Then I heard someone announce over the radio, "We have a barricade situation in the bathroom!" In preparation for this day, we had the SWAT team standing by a half-mile away in a covert location, ready to deploy if we needed them. We hadn't wanted to inflame things further by entering with them. I told my NBPD liaison to have the SWAT team get ready to deploy. Within minutes, the situation was brought under control, and the SWAT team was told to stand down.

Each detainee was taken to the immigration processing center we had set up, and extensively interviewed. For humanitarian reasons, thirty-five illegal aliens were released from MBI with an immigration order. Dozens more would follow in the days following the operation. Within the hour, the situation was well under control, and all agents were busy carrying out their assigned duties. Then I received word that the local radio station was reporting that some workers had possibly run up and over the hurricane barriers into the frigid water. I thought, *God, no!* The report back from the police vessel in the water was, "No bodies in the water." All I could do was thank the NBPD Chief for offering the police vessel.

Under my supervision, the National Security Squad, with support from nearly 300 DHS personnel and over a hundred state and local officers, had pulled off one of the largest mass arrests in U.S. history at a single location—a U.S. defense contractor. Several hundred more agents and staff were busy processing the illegal aliens at the established immigration processing center.

I thought it was a "wicked good" operation, as we say in Boston. What else could I have thought? After all, we had successfully arrested 361 illegal aliens out of 500 employees, criminally arrested the owner and two of his managers, executed a search warrant at this business, and arrested an individual producing counterfeit identifications—an individual who happened to be illegally present in the United States himself. Throughout the day, agents discovered illegal aliens hiding in boxes in the four-story brick factory where MBI was housed. The place was approximately 161,709 square feet and sat on over four acres of land, so there was no shortage of places to hide.

Feeling Betrayed in the Wicked Aftermath

On March 7, 2007, at 6:00 a.m., the morning after the "Wicked Good Raid," I heard my cell phone ringing. I had only had a few hours of sleep. It was the Special Agent in Charge (SAC), Bruce Foucart, another guy from New Bedford. Ironically, we grew up just a few streets away from each other and close to the target business. I knew that the SAC wasn't calling to congratulate me. Before heading to bed the night before, I had witnessed the beginnings of the intense media backlash. The media was claiming that MBI was a handbag plant full of women, which was patently false.

While watching *The O'Reilly Factor* (Bill O'Reilly's show on Fox News), I saw the narrative quickly turn. The raid was first described as a DOJ defense contractor/critical infrastructure/national security operation, but now it was a "humanitarian crisis," as described by the governor. I knew the case was about to go south and I was right. Now the Massachusetts Congressional Delegation was calling for a DHS Office of

Inspector General investigation on how and why the case was executed. The SAC was calling to talk to me about the raid and the blowback. During the call, the SAC said that the Department of Homeland Security was getting barraged with questions from the White House. He needed stats from me: how many males and how many females had been arrested? How many had been released from MBI for humanitarian reasons on the day of the raid? How many were released from the immigration processing center?

After spending five years working in D.C., I knew how things worked. The White House calls DHS, which then calls Immigrations & Customs Enforcement. Politics and the media were now driving the case. We had conducted our operation with oversight from the DHS, and after nearly a year of detailed planning, we had done exactly what we said we were going to do. The DHS knew perfectly well what we were setting out to do and were, in fact, in charge of it. But, because they now had to defend themselves, they went into micromanagement mode. They were picking apart our entire operation and questioning every move we had made. It was clear that their loyalties had shifted.

The SAC explained that the very same administration that was pushing for tougher immigration policies was also embarrassed that we had hit a U.S. Department of Defense contractor. The operation didn't fit the narrative of the President, and most democratic politicians, that "Illegal aliens are simply doing jobs Americans won't do." In truth, *The New Bedford Standard-Times* ran an article weeks later showing hundreds of New Bedford citizens waiting for job interviews at MBI. A prospective worker was quoted as saying "I would love to have a job with the DOD supporting our military in Iraq and Afghanistan." On the one hand, the article was coming out against our operation. On the other hand, the article supported our operation by showing New Bedford residents standing in line waiting for a job.

The illegal aliens employed by MBI came to America and entered unlawfully. They did not follow the rules required of people around the world who want to live and work in America. We are a nation of laws, and unless we want to become a third-world country, we need to enforce our laws. I understood how the desperation of the illegal aliens working at MBI drove them to break the law in hopes of living better lives. In doing so, they put themselves in a position to be exploited.

Many people said, "Well, the conditions in their homeland are worse, so this is the lesser of two evils!" I said that our immigration laws state that illegal aliens have to go back to where they came from and apply for legal entry, amnesty, or a work visa. I would add that our laws state that illegal aliens have to wait their turn, like all lawful people from around the world do, often waiting five or ten years to get to America legally.

The branch of government that employed me was in charge of enforcing our immigration laws. The system is not perfect, but we have procedures in place that have been in place for many years, and the procedures are there for valid reasons – including our safety. If our elected officials don't like these procedures, they need to change them. It is unfair to hire law enforcement officers to enforce laws and procedures and then turn on us when we do what we were hired to do.

We were hired to do a job, and we did it—with the blessing of the Department of Homeland Security!

Getting Pounded by the Wicked Aftermath

MBI had been awarded $230 million in government contracts since 2004, and the majority of its workforce were illegal foreign workers. The Defense Logistics Agency noted that MBI was one of the top defense contractors in the U.S.— number eighty-two out of one hundred, to be exact.

DOD inspectors visited MBI and even had an office on site! Insolia was quoted as saying, "Inspectors interacted with our workers without incident or complaint." The inspector did not report any labor problems because he didn't know they existed. He was told by management that the Hispanic people he saw on the factory floor were hired by an employment agency. The illegal aliens were being portrayed as victims, and they were. They had been exploited by MBI and treated like slave labor rather than human beings. Insolia was responsible for that, but the U.S. Government turned a blind eye to it. And what about the citizens of New Bedford who didn't have an opportunity for good DOD jobs? They were victims, too— the forgotten victims in the wicked aftermath.

The media, along with the local, state, and federal democratic elected officials, were all determined to set a different narrative and demonize the men and women of Homeland Security. In their eyes, this was a "wicked bad" operation, not a wicked good operation, as I believed it to be. There was even a "How dare you!" outcry from the Catholic Church. During the homilies at the masses following the Wicked Good Raid, I would hear priests pray for the undocumented workers affected by what they essentially called "the massive Nazi government raids."

Yet, I never heard one priest pray for the men and women of law enforcement. No priests prayed for me and my family or mentioned how we had sacrificed for years to keep America safe. It was fine for priests to pray for the illegal aliens, but there was no love shown for us law enforcement officers who were simply trying to enforce the laws we had sworn to enforce.

The disinformation campaign was in full swing. Meanwhile, the government held half as many press conferences as the media and did a poor job of getting out in front of the story concerning the national security implications of MBI.

It was disheartening and demoralizing to know that my own government and agency were failing to stand up for us and aggressively tell the story of what had actually occurred. They didn't come out in the media and state unequivocally that this was about national security. That was the bottom line, and that was the drum we should have been hitting from day one. Instead, we got all twisted up in the wicked aftermath. We were so busy answering the mail from the White House, the media, and the Catholic Church, so to speak, that we took our eye off the ball.

Headquarters was controlling the SAC's interaction with the media, and was operating under the naïve assumption that the media frenzy would blow over. In preparation for a pending press conference days before the operation, I had suggested to the U.S. Attorney's office that they utilize MBI Grand Jury exhibits, which included photos of the tactical flight vests manufactured by MBI and worn by U.S. fighter pilots and other servicemen in Iraq and Afghanistan. I felt that it was important that the media and public understand that national security was at the very heart of this case. Unfortunately, my advice fell on deaf ears.

I would simply ask the citizens of New Bedford this question: "Has turning a blind eye to illegal aliens, with all the residual crime and costs that flow from that, helped your city prosper over the decade? Who has it empowered, other than politicians and nongovernmental organizations?" Anyone can stand up and make great speeches, saying, "We should all be inclusive!"

Reconciling the Wicked Aftermath

Immigration advocacy groups and politicians were fabricating stories and telling half-truths about the operation. The media, an independent vital feature of any liberal democracy, must act as an effective check on government power and provide people with accurate and impartial information so they can act accordingly.

In this case, they failed miserably to uphold this tradition. *The South Coast Today* newspaper (the former *New Bedford Standard-Times*) ran front-page stories on the case for years, coming out as critical of DHS efforts. In so doing, they were unknowingly attacking the same agent they had glorified in 1998 as a "son of New Bedford who would make the forefathers of our country proud." Given that the similarities between the ESC case and the MBI case were so obvious, it was hard to believe I had been painted with such vastly different brushes by the media on these two cases.

The only real difference in the cases was that in the ESC case, the defense contractor was offshoring the production of military equipment to foreign countries, and in the MBI case, illegal foreign workers were brought to the U.S. to manufacture the goods.

Then there was the *Washington Post* article that ran on Sunday, March 18, 2007, entitled "Immigration Raid Rips Families." The article stated that someone named Maria Escoto from Honduras, who paid a "coyote" to make the fifteen-day journey to New Bedford, wasn't allowed to make a phone call for three days after her arrest, leaving her young children unaware of her whereabouts. The story went on to say that, supposedly, other children were suffering without their arrested parents as well. These included a seven-year-old who called a DHS hotline looking for her mother and a breastfeeding baby who refused a bottle and was hospitalized for dehydration. The article continued by stating that the governor categorized the raid as a humanitarian crisis. Interestingly, Ms. Escoto was quoted as saying that she was aware of similar raids but assumed that since MBI was working on government contracts, she would be "safe from a raid."

The article ended with Ms. Escoto being released with an ankle bracelet and being issued an immigration court date. The reporter failed to corroborate or contact DHS officials for comments. I always understood that the basic rule of journalism was to talk to all sides. Or, at least, that's what was preached in my journalism course at Northeastern. Evidently, this was not followed at the premier *Washington Post*. The Deputy National Editor, Steve Holmes, later admitted that failing to call officials was "a bad error on all our parts."

In fact, Ms. Escoto did make a phone call on the evening of her arrest and was released. We were never able to confirm that a seven-year-old called the established hotline or that a dehydrated baby was hospitalized. The wicked aftermath of the MBI case brought to mind this Winston Churchill quote: "A lie gets halfway around the world before the truth has a chance to get its pants on."

All these years later, I still find it astonishing that not a single news outlet asked about or investigated the national security question. Yet, at the very heart of the MBI case was our national security. If we haven't learned the most basic lesson from 9/11—the fact that terrorists are limited only by their imagination—then we, as a nation, are doomed for another attack like 9/11. Only, next time, it will be much, much worse. Let us not forget the victims of 9/11 and all those souls who have been slaughtered by terrorist groups. Let us not forget the fall of 2001 when five people died, and seventeen were sickened by anthrax.

History proves that germ warfare has been used for thousands of years. The British gave Native Americans blankets and handkerchiefs infected with smallpox. The Russians, U.S., British, and Germans all have some type of germ warfare program. If a terrorist could find his or her way into a U.S. defense contractor's facility to commit acts of sabotage, like placing a chemical nerve agent like ricin, capable of killing all whose skin it touched, why wouldn't they? Or, if terrorists were able to place tracking devices on these MBI vests so adversaries could monitor our soldiers' location and then kill them, why wouldn't they?

Who ever imagined that nineteen foreign "students" and visitors would hijack U.S. planes, kill the pilots, and fly them into our national symbols? Until it actually happened, this idea seemed foolish and crazy, something that would only happen in the imaginings of a fiction writer like Tom Clancy.

Handling the Political Machinery

I could understand the death threats I got from the MS-13 gang, the protest marches, and the rallies held, ironically, at my high school and at my family parish, St. James Church. What I found most disheartening was how the politicians—the mayor, the governor, and Senators Kennedy and Kerry—all flocked to New Bedford like ambulance-chasing lawyers, salivating over the opportunity to pose for photos with a crying baby or the child of one of the illegal aliens taken into custody. Kennedy said, "The Immigration Service performed disgracefully!"

Ironically, the best-known politician from Massachusetts, Senator Ted Kennedy—who made a guest appearance at St. James along with the mayor, state politicians, and other congressional representatives, including Senator Kerry—was in 1966 a key senator in developing and helping to pass the current immigration laws. The hypocrisy was truly unfortunate and sad.

Kerry referred to the raid as "the Bianco disgrace." Of course, this all made for great six o'clock news broadcasts and newspaper stories. But what message were they sending to the public concerning the rule of law in America—a law originally spearheaded by John F. Kennedy in 1966? It was clear to me that the media and the politicians were all working from the same script: appeal to public sympathies and demonize the U.S. Government Agents. I asked myself, *Who is feeding the beast?*

The answer to that question turned out to be MIRAC. A Carnegie Corporation case study entitled "Reframing the Immigration Debate, How the Massachusetts Immigration and Refugee Advocacy Coalition (MIRAC) Retooled its Communication Strategy" is an astonishing document. The fifteen-page undated document proved to be MIRAC's roadmap for successfully orchestrating and controlling the MBI story by directing and controlling the media and politicians who never saw a camera they didn't like. The document stated that "MIRAC's goal was to steer the story in a direction sympathetic to the arrested workers and their families."

Within hours of the operation, MIRAC called reporters and "Community leaders were identified, given talking points, and issued press advisory, immediately reframing the language of the debate from illegal workers to 'parents with children.'" They saw that the press wanted more and realized, "We have to give them a story!" So, in the first twelve days following the operation, MIRAC proudly coordinated eleven press conferences and four large rallies. MIRAC framed a March 7th press conference with a headline: "March 6: The Day That Destroyed the Immigrant Family." A decision was made not to talk about policy, so MIRAC asked themselves, "Well, what *does* move opinion and what *does* resonate? Children and mothers. That's what!"

The message was essentially, "Children are being hurt, traumatized, and separated from their parents. This resonates with the American public." MIRAC continued by stating, "When confronted with the images of crying babies, children, and mothers, almost everyone has a strong, direct, and sympathetic emotional response...it is important to find and maintain this resonance to affect the public consciousness." MIRAC's stated goal was, "to keep the coverage on the crisis strong and to give the elected officials an opportunity to enjoy positive media coverage while advocating for immigrant families." Well, there was only one problem with that statement—those immigrant families were here illegally! MIRAC was always searching for the next big story to give the media. In fact, the document stated that "the media came to see MIRAC as a credible source for continuing stories on developments and events."

On Saturday, March 10th, after seeing a MIRAC op-ed in *The Boston Globe*, I called Special Agent in Charge Bruce Foucart and practically begged him to get out in front of the media onslaught. "Otherwise," I explained, "we will lose the case in the public arena and kill the morale of the troops!" He sympathized, but told me headquarters would not let him.

The SAC did do one-off interviews weeks after the raid but it was too little too late. Then, a federal judge issued a gag order directed at him, preventing any additional interviews on the case. Malcolm X once said, "The media's the most powerful entity on earth. They have the power to make the innocent guilty and to make the guilty innocent. That's power. Because they control the minds of the masses." The media is often referred to as the fourth branch of government and responsible for reporting facts relating to the other three branches (executive, legislative, and judicial) to keep the citizens informed. In this case, the media clearly manipulated the public and colluded with MIRAC in order to advance each other's agendas.

The media's philosophy seemed to be, "Don't let the facts get in the way of a good salacious story that equals higher revenues for a dying print media!" At the end of the day, the real victims of the MBI/MIRAC media debacle were the American taxpayers, American workers, American soldiers, and the illegal aliens who were mistreated. Of course, the other victims were the agents of the DHS, myself included. We took an oath to enforce the laws of the United States formulated by elected officials and approved by our judiciary, and that was exactly what we did in the Wicked Good Raid.

Passing Around the Wicked Blame

The politicians piled on and called for congressional hearings and a "thorough" DHS investigation of the case because it was "poorly planned and executed" and caused a "humanitarian crisis." Yet, the governor's public safety head (who oversaw the Massachusetts State Police and reports directly to the governor) was thoroughly briefed every step of the way by both the SAC and myself.

The New Bedford Police Chief had also been thoroughly briefed months before and supported the investigation. He had asked the SAC and I if we could do him a favor and brief the mayor on the operation so the mayor wouldn't be blindsided, and in return, reprimand the police chief. The SAC and I had agreed, and forty-eight hours prior to the operation, on Sunday, March 4, 2007, at approximately 2:00 p.m., we traveled to meet the mayor at his residence with the chief of police. We all sat down at the mayor's dining room table, and the SAC and I identified ourselves as Special Agents with Homeland Security Investigations.

We informed the mayor that in the next few days, we were going to execute several criminal arrests and search warrants relating to a company in the City of New Bedford and that this company was knowingly hiring hundreds of illegal aliens. We told the mayor about the horrendous working conditions and informed him that hundreds of agents would be involved in this operation. The SAC explained to the mayor that this was an ongoing Grand Jury (secret) investigation and that Federal Rule 6(e) prohibited us from divulging specific target information unless approved by the court. We demanded that our briefing be kept confidential so as to not tip off the target in any way.

We went on to tell the mayor that all illegal aliens would be administratively arrested and processed and that all sole caregivers and pregnant women would be released. We stated that we were working closely with Social Services as well.

The mayor was also told that the Massachusetts Congressional Delegation in Washington, D.C. would be notified as well on the day of the operation, and we let him know that the Public Safety Secretary for the Massachusetts Governor had been briefed as well. We briefed the mayor over the course of about an hour-long conversation. As we stepped outside and were walking down his walkway toward our vehicle, the mayor stopped us and softly said to the SAC and me, "This conversation never happened." I laughed, thinking he was joking. He said, "No, I'm serious!"

I thought to myself, *How ridiculous for a former local prosecutor, a mayor, an officer of the court to make such a stupid statement to two federal agents?* What would Dad think of that? During the course of executing the search warrant simultaneously with the Wicked Good Raid, a fellow agent had asked me to come into Insolia's office and take a look at his appointment calendar. Right there in black and white was an appointment with the mayor. The mayor's words to me as I was leaving his house echoed in my head. It seemed that he knew perfectly well what was going on at MBI and had adopted an attitude of willful blindness.

Once again, I asked myself what had happened to my city. I wondered how these politicians had allowed criminal activity to go on for years at the cost of national security and employment opportunities for legal citizens. In the days, months, and years following the operation, the mayor and the governor tried their best to dance with the media concerning their knowledge of the operation. I was actually embarrassed for them, as I remembered my father always saying, "Tell the truth! People will respect you more for it."

As recently as the ten-year anniversary of the raid, the now-former mayor continued to massage the truth in an online video interview for *South Coast Today*. In that interview, after fumbling his words, the former mayor claimed he had been told that the raid was simply a labor issue. I considered his statements to be revisionist history.

About a month after the raid, I was interviewed in the office of the Special Agent in Charge by several congressional staffers. They regurgitated the same *New York Times*, *Boston Globe*, and *Washington Post* disinformation provided by MIRAC. Their presence in the office had a chilling effect, and many agents had no desire to arrest anyone now. I realized that these congressional staffers had been reading the news accounts and had already formulated the opinion that the operation was poorly planned and had harmed children. It was clear that, just like the others, they didn't care to understand the national security implications.

I felt that they wanted me to apologize for protecting our national security and for doing a job our government had hired me to do. Within a year of the Wicked Good Raid, hearings were held at the congressional and state levels. Not a word was said concerning the national security implications or of the American jobs lost to illegal aliens.

I was never reprimanded or disciplined for any perceived wrongdoing or impropriety related to the raid, nor were any of my fellow agents. From my perspective, the entire, drawn out, torturous, wicked aftermath—which dragged on for years!—was nothing more than political grandstanding designed to get the faces of democratic political officials on the six o'clock news. It was all a big show.

Time to Break out The Serenity Prayer Again

During this time, I also began to practice mixed martial arts. Besides learning self-defense, the mixed martial arts practice truly helped me understand that conflict begins and ends from within. Even in actual fights, the greatest obstacle we face is our own fear, our own breath, or our own tension.

A martial artist starts with this simple fact in mind: The battles will be won when we're willing to face ourselves. I discovered throughout my mixed martial arts training that there were many uncomfortable moments—just like there are uncomfortable days on the journey of life.

But in life, the key is to identify my limitations and work through them.

Eric Caron is the author of *Switched On - The Heart and Mind of a Special Agent* , and a U.S. government special agent and diplomat (ret.) with a decorated twenty-five-year career investigating terrorism, money laundering, and transnational crime. He is a much sought-after international speaker and contributing writer for *Voices Of Courage* magazine and other national and international publications. www.SwitchedOnLife.com

PTSD: HOW TO FACE THE UNSEEN MONSTER AND LIVE FORWARD

By Andi Buerger, JD

I felt his hand touch my left shoulder from behind. In a flash, I turned around as if to defend myself against an attacker. Instead, I saw the startled, stunned face of Robert, a good and gentle businessman who had always been kind to me whenever he came to sell his wares at my place of work. From his mouth came the words, "Whoa, who hurt you?" *If only he knew...*

It was not the first time my rigid, defensive mechanisms had kicked in over someone's genuinely innocent gesture. But what I could not understand is why, even when someone seemed safe, I had such strong physical reactions—especially if they approached from behind or the side. Just like Robert, a lot of well-meaning and "safe" people in my life inadvertently retraumatized me over the years long before counseling helped me to understand those horrifying circumstances.

By definition, Post-Traumatic Stress Disorder (PTSD) is a disorder in which a person has difficulty recovering after experiencing or witnessing a terrifying event. The condition may last months or years, with triggers that can bring back memories of the trauma accompanied by intense emotional and physical reactions. Seventeen years of child abuse, including child sex trafficking, in my life certainly provided the foundation for what has been a lifetime of managing PTSD.

As if the abuse and loss of my childhood, teen years, and early adulthood were not enough, add in ten traumatic brain injuries (TBIs), two VTach episodes, multiple surgeries including extensive hip repair, back fusion, total shoulder replacement, corrective heart surgery, Celiac disease, Ehlers-Danlos Syndrome (EDS), and Vascular EDS.

Though I was married only briefly to a classic narcissist with peculiar sexual interests, the mental and emotional battering from him took its toll. No wonder it took three solid years of weekly therapy—including a voluntary two-month residential stay to deal with dissociative disorder—and unending grace from God to get to my own personal "ground zero" from which I began building a healthier, stronger me.

As an author and international speaker, I am often asked how PTSD happens—especially by people who have not been victims of human trafficking. Most of us understand that there are residual or after-effects from any kind of physical (especially sexual), mental, and emotional abuse. Yet experiences such as a horrible car accident, a divorce (whether amicable or contentious), the death of a loved one, the loss of a job, and even seeing disturbing images on television in the news, social media, or other online platforms can cause PTSD in a person. On a larger scale, entire states and countries have suffered PTSD as a collective citizenry due to ongoing wars, civil unrest, prolonged persecution, and terrorist attacks.

To this day, I still remember the terror I felt as a five-year-old watching *The Wizard of Oz*. Flying monkeys. An evil manipulative witch. Being lost in a strange place. Battered by "high winds" (uncontrollable circumstances). All those things represented much of what I was already experiencing in my household with familial predators—especially the evil witch character. My birth mother was the orchestrator of all things evil against me and my biological brother. Now, my unsuspecting eyes saw her evil nature in a film that would last forever. The only upside in my tiny five-year-old mind was that at least the witch in the movie eventually died by melting into oblivion. The "witch" in my life took 91 years to pass from my existence.

Human beings suffering from PTSD may experience agitation, irritability, hostility, hypervigilance, self-destructive behavior, or social isolation. On some level, I still experience agitation when an activation occurs and am a bit hypervigilant about surroundings and circumstances I can, at least in part, control.

When I started professional therapy, I dealt heavily with flashbacks, the huge anxiety I faced as a working professional and abused wife, and basic distrust—which meant I had few, if any, friends because I *had* to act as if everything was "OK" in my life. I was tremendously fearful that people around me would find out that my real life was a mess, or worse—that maybe I was the cause for all the pain I endured. I had no one to share my guilt, loneliness, heartache, and nightmares with after counseling ended. No way to shelve the unwanted thoughts that crept into my mind and challenged the core of my faith-based beliefs (though never defeating them). Activities with associates or casual friends were a brief respite, but there was little, if any, joy or happiness in those encounters.

After my divorce, I desperately leaned into God's love for me. Though I felt like yesterday's garbage, God reminded me of the promise He had made to me as I attempted to take my life at the early age of five years old. He promised that I had a future and a hope. He had not forgotten me; not by a long shot.

Somehow, I knew that each and every human being has free will. It is up to that person to choose to use that free will to do good, to do evil, or to do nothing. Only one of those choices ends up producing a positive, productive, and meaningful life, though not always an easy one. My birth certificate does not say life will always be fair and every person I meet will love me. It simply says I was born. What I do with my gift of life is up to me, no matter how much others interfere with or try to squash my purpose and hope.

Years after my divorce, God brought the most amazing human I have ever known into my life. We have been married for twenty-five years now and still growing strong together. In 2008, my husband, Ed, and I founded Beulah's Place to help at-risk homeless teens find *their* future and hope in life. Our program provided temporary shelter services, food, clothing, educational assistance, job skills, employment, medical, dental, and safe cell phones for the youth we served.

Over fourteen years, we have rescued over three hundred desperate youth who ran to the streets because they were safer than what they were running from and were willing to take their chances with the night. Fifty were housed and graduated from Beulah's Place. The others received all the assistance and support we could offer to stabilize them and get resources to help them finish high school and become successful independent young adults in their communities. Twelve have either entered or graduated college and several have made the Dean's List multiple times.

Beulah's Place became the mustard seed of sorts for Voices Against Trafficking™. The success of Beulah's Place expanded our reach to help victims of human trafficking into both national and international quarters. Members of Congress from all sides joined our fight for the rights of innocents to live safe and free with resources to support their health and welfare.

I have heard the best and the worst from helping at-risk youth get back on their feet. Sometimes, the stories and circumstances surrounding these teens, and even the volunteers who housed and worked with them, activate my own past traumas. Though I am not completely proficient at it, I work every day to sharpen my self-care tools and continue creating that safe, nurturing support system for times when the overwhelm is—well—overwhelming.

Things that have helped me personally include reducing the "noise" in my life for a period of time, whether it be less music, television, or activities—and just being still. I find a spot in the house or outdoors where I work on "quietness" from within. Sometimes, I reach out by text or email to a friend if I feel I can't call and speak about it. When it's deeply affecting me, I reach out to my core support (husband, daughter, pastor, lifetime and best friends). Every now and then, I engage in what I call maintenance counseling, a time to just check in on my own personal management of "me," particularly where emotional, mental, and physical stress loads seem to be colliding with each other.

It is critical for any human being to learn to love who they are from the inside out. But those who have been so deeply hurt may not know or remember what real love is or means. So it is a huge challenge as a society to not simply judge another person by their projected image.

In both my own experiences and those of the ones I have had the honor of rescuing, trauma victims carry a *huge* load. One of the best remedies is to allow each victim to be who they are in that moment without judgment or platitudes. **Look** for signs of distress. Find books and articles about PTSD and get familiar with the "tell" signs. **Listen** to what the person who has been traumatized is relaying to you, whether it seems like a big deal to you or not. Everybody has a different level of pain tolerance. The recovery process can be short or long, but PTSD has no known cure. The cause of PTSD in someone's life would have to be completely undone or erased, which is not possible. Even in hidden memories, the trauma exists.

Many trauma victims use journals, exercise, special treats like lunches out, or certain perks that bring them joy and happiness. These are the healthier ways to practice self-care. Most important is for victims at any age—especially children—to have a safe support system, whether it involves family or not. As a supporter, be available. When a trauma victim reaches out, it is because they are experiencing a trauma you cannot see in most cases. Witnessing an accident has an immediate impact on bystanders and those involved. Both groups could have long-lasting trauma, or they might simply move on. Those who have been abused or trafficked will never have that option. The trauma lasts for a lifetime. The quality of life depends on the choices both the victim and the community around the victim provide to each other.

After six decades, I finally acknowledged publicly that I struggle with PTSD. My extensive coping mechanisms have allowed me to be successful on many fronts. In 2019, I began having periods of not feeling like "me," and I wondered where "I" had gone. Sometimes, these periods were very brief, and other times, they were not. I struggled with triggers I could not identify and started searching for anything within me that might need to surface. As I work through these events, I realize that I am capable of allowing more healing, more love for myself so I can heal, and a more dedicated quest to help others—especially victims of human trafficking—find the same things for their lives. *Every* human being is valuable. *Every* human being deserves the right to find their unique future and hope.

Andi Buerger, JD is Founder of Voices Against Trafficking™. Her books *Voices Against Trafficking*™ - *The Strength of Many Voices Speaking As One* and *A Fragile Thread of Hope: One Survivor's Quest to Rescue* are available on Amazon.com. Her *Voices of Courage* magazine is available online at *Voices* of Courage.media with a television program, also titled *Voices of Courage,* due out in 2026. Andi's work continues to appear in numerous publications, books, online news outlets, and bestselling titles including *Everyday Triumph - Extraordinary Stories of Hope, Resilience, and Impact,* by Chris Meek, Ed.D.

TO MODEL OR NOT TO MODEL? KNOW THE RISKS
By Pamela Privette

In any industry, education is the first step to ensuring your safety. This includes the modeling and fashion worlds. You must do your own due research. Do not get caught up in your dream!

As an award-winning producer in the fashion industry and the mother of a successful, professional model, I know the path to a modeling career is challenging and has both risks and coveted rewards.

There are many professional agencies, agents, photographers, production companies, and runways in the business. Unfortunately, the multi-billion dollar industry of fashion does not have one centralized place for consumers to check the credibility and legitimacy of a company or person you could be dealing with in your journey to success. The dreams of "the beautiful life" leave many hopefuls vulnerable and losing money along the way.

No one goes out to purchase a high-asset investment without doing research. The same holds true for the fashion industry. To become a professional model, it requires an investment in your craft. Just as in any career—sports, music, ballet, gymnastics—preparation is required. Taking selfies and posting them on social media will not get you there. You will only receive vanity likes and comments and attract potential predators who troll the internet looking for easy prey, such as a photographer reaching out and asking to set up a photoshoot with you.

Remember, the internet has no safety mechanism. You have no idea who you are really dealing with—and this warning goes out to both genders. If you want to do the shoot, ask questions. For example, what is the photographer's website? Do they have references? (Be sure to check them!) What is the address of the shoot location?

Can you bring an escort with you? If they say no, don't go! Is there a dressing facility for a change of clothing? Will hair and makeup be provided? What's the pricing for the shoot? Do you have a contract and licensing for the photos? These things are very important, as you don't want to get into a lawsuit!

Never shoot in a hotel room. No nudes. Do not go to remote locations. Let me repeat this: *no nudes*, and do not go to remote locations. When I say no nudes, I mean no buttocks, no breasts, nothing revealing at all! If you do, then you put yourself in a specific area of the industry.

Let's say your dream is to be a runway model. I would like to point out that the main fashion weeks are only twice a year. The ones that pay the most are in the Big Four of fashion: New York City, Milan, London, and Paris. You can also do showroom modeling or other modeling in submarkets, but you must diversify your skills into other parts of the industry to stay employed full-time. This is common for other professions as well. Almost every actor, for instance, also dances, sings, or plays an instrument.

Once again, do your research. How long has the fashion show production company been in business? Ask for references and check them out. Is there a preparation fee? Is there a private dressing room for models? How long are you required to attend during the event? Are photographers allowed back in the dressing room? Photographers should not be allowed backstage! Look at the company's video content and the photographers used and pay attention to *everything*.

Never feel embarrassed about checking references and asking questions. You have a right to know the answers. If the company is legitimate, they will answer your questions. But remember, as I tell all models, "You do not come to the New York Fashion Week, Milan, Paris, or London to learn how to model. This is where you showcase your modeling." This is the Super Bowl of modeling. Get prepared prior to coming to Fashion Week. Don't be surprised if hiTechMODA doesn't ask you for your Instagram handle. Potential models should have a walking video on all their social media sites!

I do not want to discourage you from following your dreams and goals; just know that there are real dangers out there, and some are grave dangers (such as human trafficking). You must be smart and not get caught up in the glamor of becoming a model. To be a professional model is very demanding and requires dedication. It's not just being a model when you are in front of the camera.

A professional model is a lifestyle, which means twenty-four hours a day, seven days a week. Go after your goals—but please, please be smart about it. My daughter, Paige, has been a professional New York City model for over seven years. Her career has expanded to include the Washington, D.C. area. She is a working model, and yes, it is lucrative. She has the clout of being a professional model, but once again, it is a lifestyle choice. I was on the journey with her when she began her career. It *can* be done.

Pamela Privette is CEO of the independent, award-winning fashion production company hiTechMODA. www.hitechmoda.com

HEALING REQUIRES SAFETY
By K. L. Byles

If you had told me a few months ago that human trafficking is a multi-billion dollar global evil ensnaring men, women, and children into a web of forced labor and sex slavery, I would have thought you guilty of a dark imagination influenced by a James Bond movie. I still reel from the moment I first heard about the number of victims, some 600,000-800,000 per year worldwide—only an estimate of the depth of the depravity. What happens to these people after they are finally freed from bondage? Why aren't shelters overflowing? The answer is: *they are*.

The lack of physical accommodation for survivors of human trafficking immediately upon rescue is a known and recognized issue among those involved with the prevention of human trafficking and the care of survivors. According to the National Human Trafficking Statistics Hotline, in 2021, 10,360 cases of human trafficking were identified in the U.S., with 16,710 victims of sex and labor trafficking arising from these cases. In some instances, young survivors are forced to spend time in a juvenile detention facility because there is no safe house or appropriate accommodations at all. Imagine escaping one prison for another.

According to Saint Francis Ministries, 2,100 beds are available in the U.S. for survivors of human trafficking. These accommodations range from emergency or temporary shelter to long-term housing, with 86.7% for female survivors, less than 1% for minor male survivors, 12.5% for mixed genders, and no beds at all for adult male survivors. Nine states in the U.S. reported *no* accommodations whatsoever. Groups dedicated to aiding the homeless and victims of domestic violence often provide beds to survivors of human trafficking, but human trafficking survivors have needs that only an organization devoted to them is equipped to provide.

I spoke with Adam Kavanaugh, a trainer for caregivers of survivors of child exploitation and sex trafficking and a retired Sergeant of the St. Louis County Police Department, and Cindy Malott, a Professional Trainer and CSE/HT Response Consultant, Director of U.S. Safe Programs, Crisis Aid International. Mr. Kavanaugh cautioned about focusing on statistics because of the lack of trustworthy numbers concerning human trafficking. Commenting about the number of beds, "As a general rule, there is not enough." This lack of accommodation often leads to further exploitation and trauma.

Ms. Malott noted, "I can't tell you how many times it's been in the middle of the night, I have a young person who needs somewhere safe to go, and there is nothing available." In many cases, this young person has been sold out of a hotel, and to tell them they will be put in a hotel room is devastating. Plus, a hotel offers no support for this young person. Crisis Aid now has a shelter in St. Louis and is in the process of building another in the Grand Rapids area.

Upon rescue, per Ms. Malott added, a survivor of human trafficking has unique needs, including trauma-informed care. A homeless shelter or domestic violence shelter is not equipped to adequately house and care for these individuals who have experienced "child sexual abuse, domestic violence, possibly abuse and neglect, human trafficking, sexual assault, multiple sexual assaults." It's "a complex web of trauma, and it's just not something that can be responded to in the same way as ... a one-time incident of something or one type of traumatic experience, such as intimate partner violence." The victim needs specific case management, advocacy, and support to move forward into a stable situation and achieve healing. The staff needs experience working with trafficking survivors.

Of those referred to Crisis Aid, Ms. Malott revealed that, 90% have experienced child sexual abuse prior to trafficking, 80% have been in foster or adoptive care, about 35% have a developmental or intellectual disability, and a higher percentage have a learning disability. The greatest risk is the inexperience of the youth themselves, with the average age of child sex trafficking survivors at 14.5 years and 21 for adults. In her experience, the adults in the safe house are often 18-19 years old, with most survivors being young females. "There's definitely no housing or shelter for the other demographics because there's not enough for that (young females), and that's the primary demographic we see." According to Saint Francis Ministries, of the beds available nationwide, 62.6% are for adults only, leaving 37.4% for minors. As a mother and grandmother, I cannot imagine what these young people have endured only to be left to fend for themselves upon rescue or placed in a facility ill-equipped to care for them.

To combat the threat to youngsters, Mr. Kavanaugh and Ms. Malott developed the Children's Anti-exploitation Partnership (CAP). This organization is dedicated to not only aiding young survivors of sex trafficking but also drawing on Mr. Kavanaugh's law enforcement background and Ms. Malott's advocacy experience, preventing victimization and revictimization of children through education. CAP trains school staff, parents, and children on how to prevent predation and grooming, especially online.

Per Ms. Malott, they have found that 76% of sales of underage girls are initiated online. CAP is a mentoring program designed to build self-esteem, promote critical thinking concerning healthy relationships, and improve the understanding of healthy boundaries. CAP is available in the St. Louis and Grand Rapids areas with plans to expand. Both Ms. Malott and Mr. Kavanaugh expressed their hope to have this program available in every city in the U.S. that does not have an effective program in place. CAP will also teach this model to other organizations.

Here in Southwest Virginia, we have one of the few shelters designed for survivors of human trafficking. Melissa Gaona is the Communications Coordinator for The Lampstand, located in Roanoke, VA. She is also a journalist and news anchor at WDBJ, the local CBS affiliate station. The Lampstand is a faith-based nonprofit offering a safe home for girls twelve to seventeen years of age, but the organization does not discriminate in any way based on the faith of the survivor. The Lampstand offers trauma-informed care. Ms. Gaona remarked, "When it comes to human trafficking, you really have to have a space where they (survivors) can go where the trauma from exploitation and human trafficking, sexual abuse, is specifically addressed. Without addressing that trauma, we know that victims and survivors will go back to their traffickers at least *seven* times before actually leaving."

I gaped at this statement, but Ms. Gaona explained this is due to the similarities between domestic violence and trafficking. In both instances, the person is not held captive, but they are reluctant to leave their abuser or trafficker due to a psychological or trauma hold. Often, as in the case of domestic violence, the trafficker is a relative, spouse, or boyfriend. The victim is resistant to leave and will return unless given the proper care and resources. In many cases, the Lampstand is not the first stop for survivors due to the need for recovery from drug addiction. Because The Lampstand houses children, residents cannot have a violent criminal record. For those who cannot be housed due to age or other considerations, The Lampstand offers wraparound services, including mentoring and education. There are no prerequisites or prior expectations to enter this program.

Speaking of human trafficking, Ms. Gaona said, "People have to be educated on what it is, how to spot it, how to report it, and what it could potentially look like. I believe that almost every single day, we pass a victim of human trafficking or sexual exploitation. I just don't think we know what to do." This is why the Lampstand goes into schools to train children to prevent their victimization.

For those wanting to aid survivors in their community, Ms. Malott recommended researching local organizations and then contacting them to learn their needs, such as for volunteers, construction, or fundraising. She mentioned people often want to interact with the survivors, but this is not always healthy for them due to the need for privacy and healing. Offering to shop for birthday items by contacting staff and getting suggestions, even though one may never meet the young person, frees up hours of the staff members' time.

Ms. Gaona observed that most safe homes close after three years due to lack of funding, *retraumatizing* survivors left without housing or resources. The Lampstand originally opened its doors debt-free and with three years of funding available. Emmagail Bowers, Communications Specialist for The Lampstand, shared a statement from Rebecca Bruno, Program Director at The Lampstand's safe home. Ms. Bruno provided her vision of the future for survivors of human trafficking. "For juveniles in Virginia, I think we need a step before The Lampstand, a 90-day lockdown facility, especially for those coming straight out of a trafficking situation. They need more security for added safety." She continued, "For our seventeen to eighteen-year-olds, after completing our program, I would love to see something like a protected community of mini homes, where we provide free housing, help survivors find jobs, enroll at community college, establish bank accounts, have survivor-led support groups, etc. Independent living with support." The Lampstand is available to create a training curriculum for any organization at no cost.

I thank God there are people dedicated to aiding the survivors of human trafficking. Ms. Malott emphasized we need to learn how to *prevent* human trafficking, not just respond to it. More needs to be done. More shelters designed to meet the unique needs of these victims, some only children, need to be established to rebuild the spirits of survivors and provide the care they require and deserve. As Ms. Malott stated, "There needs to be safety in healing for survivors."

K. L. Byles is an author, editor, and writing coach. www.linkedin.com/in/kimbylesauthor

COMBATING HUMAN TRAFFICKING: TACKLING DEMAND WITH FEDERAL ACCOUNTABILITY
By Chris Meek, Ed.D

Human trafficking currently remains one of the most egregious violations of human rights. It's a global blight that preys on the most vulnerable, exploiting fifty-million men, women, and children through modern slavery in the forms of forced labor and forced sexual servitude. Despite significant legislative efforts across the United States and other countries around the world to address trafficking, it remains a $150 billion industry according to the International Labour Organization with such high demand that often undermines legislative measures.

There are a vast array of variables to take into account when looking to combat the heinous impacts of human trafficking in the United States, including the tragic situation playing out at our country's southern border and the root causes for immigration from many countries around the world. However, to truly combat human trafficking, the United States must also focus on including demand reduction in its efforts through a shift in approach that adds a federal layer of intervention to laws already on the books in states and municipalities.

Without regular demand for commercial sex, which is driven almost entirely by men, there would be no market for traffickers to exploit. According to the 2019 Demand Abolition Report, this demand often occurs in high frequency, meaning that 25% of buyers are actively doing so on a regular basis and account for 75% of all purchases.

As it stands, trafficking is already a federal crime due to its cross-border nature. However, the prostitution of trafficked individuals is not uniformly addressed at the federal level. This gap allows buyers to evade significant consequences for the trafficking component, thereby perpetuating the cycle of exploitation. Though the rights of individual states are paramount to ensuring that local issues are addressed properly and designed to protect individuals, we ought to consider that just as immigration and interstate commerce have always been and will always be proper federal policy areas, trafficking - which is naturally related to both immigration policy and interstate commerce—should also carry a federal burden.

In 2003, Washington became the first state to criminalize human trafficking, setting a precedent that every state has since followed with its own set of laws. While these laws are crucial in prosecuting traffickers, they vary widely in terms of definitions, penalties, enforcement, and effectiveness. This patchwork system presents a unique set of challenges, particularly when addressing the demand side of the trafficking equation.

Currently, the criminalization of buying sex varies significantly from state to state (and even locality to locality). Some states impose severe penalties for sex purchasers, treating them similarly to traffickers, while others apply lesser charges. This inconsistency complicates the fight against trafficking and fails to create a unified deterrent for those seeking to exploit individuals. To combat this effectively, a federal component to penalizing demand is an approach that could be considered.

To address this without compromising current state laws or violating states' rights, federal legislation should specifically target the buying of sex from trafficked individuals. Under this proposed legislation, a person found purchasing sex from someone who turns out to be a trafficked individual would become eligible for a federal charge of human trafficking. This would not only increase the stakes for buyers but also create a strong deterrent against exploiting trafficked individuals.

Such a law could be modeled after the principles underlying federal hate crimes legislation. In cases where federal hate crime statutes are applied, an individual may face additional federal charges from those at the state level if their crime is motivated by bias. Similarly, buyers of sex from trafficked individuals could face federal charges, irrespective of their knowledge of the trafficking situation. This dual-layered approach—state charges for prostitution and federal charges for trafficking—would enhance the deterrent effect and bring greater accountability to those fueling the demand.

A federal mandate would streamline the legal process, ensuring that all states adhere to a unified standard when it comes to penalizing buyers of sex from trafficked individuals. This uniformity is crucial in creating a coherent national strategy to tackle trafficking. By making federal charges applicable in cases involving trafficked persons, we address the disparity in state laws and bring a higher level of scrutiny and consequence to those who perpetuate the demand for commercial sex. Since immigration and interstate commerce are both well established as legitimate areas of federal policy, the rights of states are not compromised.

The beauty of this proposal lies in its bipartisan appeal. There is no partisan divide in the fundamental belief that trafficking is a heinous crime. Both Democratic and Republican legislators can rally behind this solution that addresses this issue head-on, as it aligns with both moral imperatives and practical concerns about human rights and justice.

Reducing demand through federal penalties for buyers of sex from trafficked individuals is not only a novel idea, but also a practical solution to a persistent problem. It provides a clear path to reducing the market that traffickers exploit and sends a powerful message that such crimes will not be tolerated in the United States. By holding buyers accountable at the federal level, we can significantly weaken the trafficking industry and move closer to eradicating this atrocity from our society.

Chris Meek, Ed.D was at Ground Zero on September 11, 2001, and in its aftermath founded SoldierStrong, a national nonprofit dedicated to helping veterans take their next steps forward by donating revolutionary medical technologies to VA medical centers across the country. He is also the founder of Frontline Foundation, which advocates for the health and rights for America's first responders. Bestselling author and television host, he resides in Stamford, CT with his wife and three children.

LACK OF FINANCIAL AND HUMAN RESOURCES FUELS HUMAN TRAFFICKING, SEXUAL EXPLOITATION, AND ILLEGAL IMMIGRATION WORLDWIDE

By Randy Purham

A retired United States Army Sergeant First Class (SFC) and United States House of Representatives candidate for the great state and "The Last Frontier" of Alaska, my military career has spanned twenty-two years as a Chemical Operations Specialist, including three tours to Iraq. During my last three years in the military, I have had the esteemed privilege to serve at Joint Force Command Naples (JFC-Naples) in the North Atlantic Treaty Organization (NATO) based out of Naples, Italy.

It was a unique assignment, and I am very honored to have gained so many friends from the international community as well as the opportunity to travel to various countries, meeting and seeing so many other people and places. I am a very strong advocate for victims of human trafficking and have spent some time discussing these issues at length in political circles and while serving in the military, particularly in Fort Hood, Texas, where human sex trafficking rings were quite prevalent and still are to this very day[19].

Human trafficking struck close to home for me a few years back when I learned a former colleague of mine was arrested for his participation in a sex trafficking prostitution ring. Fort Hood is littered with stories of human and sex trafficking; however, this one story resonated with me because my colleague (Seymore) was someone I considered a friend and never thought would be involved in anything of this nature.

While I was stationed in Anchorage, Alaska, from 2012-2015, the "asylum," or Refugee Placement Program, conducted by the Obama Administration brought many Somalians to the United States. Some were brought to Alaska and scattered throughout Anchorage's less affluent areas. While these areas were already prime locations for sex work activity by natives and other minority groups living in the area, it was exacerbated by the influx of Somalian refugees who were seeking to make ends meet in the austere conditions in a foreign place.

According to research done by the Center for Immigration Studies (CIS) between October 2000 and September 2016, "97,447 Somali refugees were admitted during that period. Most are Muslims (99.7 percent), rather young (77.44 percent are under 31 years old and 55.55 under 21 years old), with very little education (91 percent either primary or less; only 1 percent with some sort of college/university). The top five resettlement states are Minnesota, Texas, Ohio, New York, and Arizona."[20].

---

19 Corey Dickstein, "More than a dozen Fort Hood soldiers arrested in Texas prostitution ring," *Stars and Stripes*, last modified September 7, 2017
20 Nayla Rush, "Somali Refugees in the US: Terrorists Have Families Too," *Center For Immigration Studies*, last modified December 12, 2016, https://cis.org/Rush/Somali-Refugees-US

During the Obama administration, a total of 294 Somalian refugees were resettled in Anchorage, Alaska[21]. It's very rare to find yourself in a conversation, or within earshot of conversations, about refugee victims of trafficking, sex rings, and even coerced terrorist operations. These kinds of conversations raise too many eyebrows and place a sense of fault or guilt on government officials who participate in these resettlement programs with unintended consequences.

During this period, I served not only in the military but also as the Junior Vice Commander for the Veterans of Foreign Wars (VFW) Post 10252 and as an Ambassador for the Anchorage Chamber of Commerce. In conversations with community leaders, we sought solutions to curb the growth of issues that stemmed from missing (abducted) children and adults and the exploitation of vulnerable individuals such as high school students. Our efforts seemingly went unheard or were brushed off as low-priority due to the vast number of other issues that consumed the media during this time. There was also the impression that any effort to tackle these issues would result in more work than anyone was willing to deal with.

Sex work was not only a taboo discussion—in many circles, it was an acceptable form of work that was handled by consenting adults. Or at least this is what it was relegated to. What folks failed to realize was while sex is something held between mutually consenting adults, whether in exchange for something or not, there were innocent children that were part of this world of sex trafficking, organ harvesting, and human trafficking to other countries such as Russia and China.

---

21 "Somali Resettlement Figures," *Tallahassee Democrat*, last modified December 31, 2019, https://data.tallahassee.com/refugee/alaska/somalia/all/

Sadly, no one during these years was equipped to handle this reality and considered it as "something to be looked into." Whatever that meant. Alaska has long been considered the most dangerous state for women. Unfortunately, that misnomer has now grown to include nearly the entire United States as more and more cases of abductions, rapes, and murders grow among the southern border states. The policies of the Biden Administration, with gross negligence and dereliction of duty by Department of Homeland Security Secretary Alejandro Mayorkas, have only exacerbated the problem.

In my time stationed in Naples, Italy, I was exposed to a stark reality that I would only have seen on television or heard through conversations about foreign affairs: human trafficking conducted in broad daylight with hardly anyone batting an eye to what was unfolding right in front of them. Sadly, it boiled down to the sex trafficking of migrant women, mainly coming from African countries. Prostitution in Italy is LEGAL. It is in Germany as well, where you will find this activity highly regulated and contained in brothels located in cities like Frankfurt, Munich, and smaller surrounding cities close to military installations—commonly also known as "Red Light Districts."

In 2017, my family and I were relocated to Naples, Italy. We arrived in early summer, just in time to get adjusted to the weather. Air conditioning is considered a luxury there, so not many places off the military installation would have it. Opened windows and a lot of water were the key to survival in temperatures exceeding 75 degrees. We often took walks down by the Bay of Naples, an area that has a coastline stretching across the downtown area. It is a popular area to hop on a boat or ferry after a day of shopping and enjoy lunch on one of the neighboring islands, such as Capri or Ischia.

While it was customary to do these things, it was also customary to pay—seemingly by force—the African male attendants that sat in the parking lots of the public attractions. This payment, typically around five euros, was to ensure the safety of your vehicle and guarantee that everything would be intact upon your return. Even in broad daylight, your windows could be busted out, tires flattened or removed, and the inside of the vehicle vandalized. Amazingly, no one would see a thing!

Cheap Americans are the target of these heinous attacks. The African males who work these parking lots know the difference between touring Americans and regular local Italians. If an American is accompanied by an Italian, you have a 75% chance of being ok. Overall, it is just easier to pay the African the change, recommended to be kept in the center console or somewhere in the vehicle to avoid being a victim.

You may ask, why African males? Why are they doing these things? As African migrants/immigrants/trafficked persons come into the country, they are not arriving with many personally acquired resources. In fact, many, if not all, have their resources taken upon arrival by exploiters for safe passage and guarantees of "freedom" from being deported or detained. Personal identification records are taken, and a ransom or fee (up to 10,000 euros) is the debt they incur to be truly free from their exploiter's captivity.

Males are then left to work in farms and field harvesting, parking lots, or if they're lucky, a laborious industry such as cleaning stores or minor street construction. Of course, these men are paid less than normal or desirable wages and they are paid under the table to avoid payroll and taxes. Many businesses will not hire them for two reasons: 1) They are migrants—legal status in question. 2) They are typically undocumented. These two factors alone would place business owners in a precarious position if they took such a risk of being associated with Africans.

Female African arrivals have it far worse. They are mostly relegated to working the streets as prostitutes or working as maids. Living options for females are typically either with their exploiters or in secluded (out of sight, but easy to find if you're looking) trailer parks or makeshift shacks. Often, you will find them holding up residence in abandoned buildings and warehouses, unbothered by local authorities.

These women, among those of other nationalities, are transported around towns neighboring the city of Naples to work the wooded or vegetated areas where passersby can easily pick them up and return them to the location in a matter of minutes, all the while being under surveillance by someone on a bike or a parked car in the event there's trouble, or the woman is gone longer than expected. On the surface, one might think these women enjoy their line of work, as you can also find groups of them in stores shopping together for makeup and outfits. They are not very social with others outside of their groups as they are under the microscope, and any hint of trying to seek help or get away is a futile task to undergo. After speaking with local authorities and some local friends that I had made, my curiosity about this covert yet overt operation grew. The issue had piqued my interest. Aside from the tactics and procedures I previously mentioned, there is another dynamic I have not discussed: the exploiters.

The exploiters come from a variety of backgrounds. They are your everyday average citizen who may work a typical 9-5 job, someone considered a domestic engineer (house-spouse), or a stay-at-home relative. When you hear the term Mafia or Street Gang, you may immediately think of elaborate networks of people with fancy cars, homes, and clothing. No. Far from it.

The mafia members that I have encountered were simple people like a bakery worker, a janitor, a local police officer, and a schoolteacher.

The prostitution "game" is only a pillar in which money is made and favors are given. Exploiting vulnerable women is considered a win-win situation for both the exploited and the exploiter. For example, a schoolteacher may have access to a few women. He dials into the handlers to acquire them, pays a fee for the exchange, and takes the women to work for him or someone else. They all get paid. The schoolteacher then returns the women back to the handler, profiting off the proceeds the women have made from their work.

Often, the transactions are split in an agreed-upon ratio, like 70-30. Exploiters do not stay in this business for long. Especially ones with careers or families. They will do it for a couple of years before passing on their knowledge and network to the new guy or gal that comes along. It is a vicious and never ending cycle. "The supply will always be available, and so will the demand," one person mentioned in a briefing he provided to my colleagues and me during a discussion about the missing and exploited people around Southern Italy.

Rescue boats and human aid vessels are some of the biggest means used to bring migrants/immigrants/trafficked persons into any European coastal country. For example, in Palermo, Italy, in 2017, a German aid group had a boat full of migrants that was seized by the Italian coastguard for aiding in illegal immigration[22]. While this story is one of the larger operations

---

22 Wladimiro Pantaleone, "Italy Seizes NGO Rescue Boat for Allegedly Aiding in Illegal Immigration," *Reuters*, https://www.reuters.com/article/us-europe-migrants-italy-ngo/italy-seizes-ngo-rescue-boat-for- allegedly-aiding-illegal-migration-idUSKBN1AI21B

that was intercepted by authorities, there are dozens more that go undetected or hardly mentioned involving smaller boats and smaller groups of people.

Many of these smaller groups are subsequently let off the hook or let into the country due to a lack of resources to facilitate a safe return to their country of origin. Although African migrants are the largest population of exploited and trafficked persons in the European sector, independent sex workers from other neighboring countries find themselves victimized in similar fashions.

Women travel to "prostitution-permitting countries" in search of opportunity, to have a new life, or to get away from dire situations in their home countries. Unable to afford the relocation costs, many turn to independent sex work, where they prostitute without the "protection" of traffickers. These women find themselves in trouble with territorial issues or customers who may be a bit too aggressive for their liking. They then turn to exploiters for help and fall into the trap of being "forever indebted" to their exploiter or, as they call them, their *protector*.

A lack of resources—both financial and human—is one of the biggest deficits in combating human trafficking, sexual exploitation, and illegal immigration in countries like the United States, Mexico, Italy, France, and Germany. Foreign policy responses to these situations have also been lackluster in terms of addressing an end-all solution to curbing these activities.

The prevailing arguments and reasons for these deficits are that politicians, as well as local, state, and federal authorities, have benefited, either financially or through other means, by allowing or participating in these activities at the expense of those seeking to migrate from one place to another. It is unfortunate that this allegedly taboo discussion is not being addressed in a meaningful way, with serious and honest dialogue about what is happening and how to fix it. But that would require someone in the room, someone sitting at the table, to take ownership of the fact that, by their action or inaction, they have exacerbated the problem to the levels we see in the present moment. We hear of the perpetrator(s) who were arrested for soliciting or trafficking but never ever hear of the connected network that was involved or enabled this "end product" to exist in the first place being taken down. Why is that?

There are dozens of organizations, resources, and communities specially designed to help combat human trafficking, and there are many support groups and advocacy programs like Voices Against Trafficking™ that exist to assist survivors of this egregious crime against humanity. A colleague of mine, Jon Uhler, has a website (www.survivorsupport.net) that has a plethora of resources available to those who have experienced or know someone who has experienced traumatic events such as being trafficked, raped, or otherwise abused in any form. We as the human community must do more to stand up, speak out, and apply serious pressure to our governmental leaders to do more and put an end to human trafficking and exploitation of persons.

While I was serving in the military, there were two frequent sayings we would always hear when it came to accountability: "See something, say something," and "Silence is compliance." As the reader of this book today, I hope that you were inspired by my experiences to go forth and be a warrior for the exploited, be an advocate for the voiceless, and be a source of healing for the hurt. We can no longer use naïvite as an excuse for our inaction. It is time to fight. We all have three choices in life when it comes to dealing with hard issues that face us: give in, give up, or give it all you got. I hope and pray you sincerely give it all you got.

Randy Purham has a Bachelor's in Business Administration from American Military University and is a Political Science grad student. He enlisted into the U.S. Army in 1998 and has completed five campaigns in three tours to Iraq and one to Kuwait in support of Operation Enduring Freedom. Currently, he is an Internet TV Host of *The NEW w/Randy and April* for The Exceptional Conservative Network (TECN) www.tecntv.com. His personal philosophy behind everything he does is inspired by Zig Ziglar, "If you help enough people get everything they need, you'll have everything you need."

BUILDING BRIDGES: TURNING WHAT WAS MEANT FOR EVIL INTO GOOD

By Casandra Diamond and Mikhaela Gray-Beerman

There may be content in this chapter that could potentially trigger some readers. Please use discretion if you have been sexually exploited, trafficked, or sexually abused.

Introduction[23]

My story is not an easy one to tell. In fact, every time I tell my story, I am retraumatized. But if sharing my story means that one more girl has a chance at freedom, then it is worth it for me.

Growing up in my family was not easy. Mental health problems and abuse can destabilize a family. In my case, these mental health problems and this abuse led to neglect, and neglect left me on the streets of Scarborough as a very young girl. One summer, I was raped by a stranger; another summer, I was abused and degraded by the neighborhood boys. I was always in fight-

---

23   The text in the introduction first appears in a TED x Toronto by Casandra Diamond entitled: 'I was sex trafficked for years; brothels are hidden in plain sight | Casandra Diamond."

or-flight mode. It seemed like danger was lurking around every corner. I would later be abused at the hands of a multi-generational pedophile. It was his words that kept me trapped. When he said, "Your parents won't love you anymore if you tell on me," in my isolated environment, I believed him. My behaviors started to reflect the environment that I lived in. I do not remember a time back then when my body *ever* felt like my own.

At the age of seventeen, I started moving from club to club. I first started stripping. Then later, I worked for a smut magazine where I would meet some of the most dangerous people I have ever encountered. Still, I was on this never ending quest to have some form of agency over my own body, a source of power that I had never had before.

One day, my phone rang. I was looking at my gas gauge, sitting on empty. It was my old coworker from the magazine company. He called me to tell me he was running Toronto's largest massage parlor, and he wanted me to come and join his stable[24]. On the outside, it looked like a normal business, except that it wasn't. This massage parlor had ten rooms, and they were always busy. There were between forty to sixty women and girls on rotation in the spa. A massage was between forty and fifty dollars. We would get a ten-dollar commission if we didn't receive a fine. You could be given a fine for just about anything—being late, talking back, or not having a perfectly primped body. It was expected that the girls could earn considerably more money by doing "extras," which meant engaging in some of the most unimaginable and degrading acts. This was my life for the next nearly ten years.

---

[24] "Stable" refers to a group of women under the control of a third-party actor.

I was told how to dress, who to have sex with, where to live, everything. I felt scared almost all of the time. The man who recruited me manipulated me into thinking and believing that he was my protector and my boyfriend—except that he wasn't. He was my trafficker, and I was little more than his property. This is what sex trafficking looks like in Canada.

I eventually escaped my circumstances. I literally slept for three days straight. Discovering my faith in a supportive community guided me to seek counseling, where my journey to recovery began. Getting out of the sex industry is one thing, but staying out is just as hard. It is with this understanding that I started BridgeNorth. I want to be a part of the solution.

Sex Trafficking, Technology, and Online Exploitation

The trafficking of persons is a growing problem around the globe, and the internet plays a significant role. The U.S. National Human Trafficking Hotline reports that the internet is the top recruitment location for all forms of trafficking[25]. The internet has made youth more accessible to perpetrators, 24 hours a day, seven days a week. Cybertip.ca, Canada's national tip line for reporting the online sexual exploitation of children, states that there has been an 815% increase in online sexual luring of Canadian kids over the past five years[26]. Deception is more difficult to detect in online spaces, and it is not possible to verify that the person behind the screen is who they say they are.

---

25 January Contreras, "Technology's Complicated Relationship With Human Trafficking," The Administration for Children and Families, 2022, https://acf.gov/archive/blog/2022/07/technologys-complicated-relationship-human-trafficking.
26 Cybertip.ca, 2023, https://www.cybertip.ca/en/campaigns-and-media/news-releases/2023/safer-internet-day-2023/

Adults can communicate and access youth online from anywhere in the world, which has significantly impacted sex trafficking, including lowering the age of those who are exploited. Social media and the internet are vehicles for younger and younger people to be exploited. In Canada, 78% of child sexual abuse materials on the internet depict children under twelve, with the majority of those being under the age of eight years[27]. Children are being lured, groomed, and exploited through the internet at alarming rates.

In previous decades, youth would typically go to school and return home. If someone wanted to meet with a youth, they would have to connect face-to-face. As a result of technology, the sex industry has become less visible. Today, youth can receive a message on an electronic device to meet a stranger down the street. While children are sitting at their houses, at school, or at various places in the community, they can receive a text message or a call from a trafficker and can be instructed to go out to a specific car or location where the sexual transaction will take place. Additionally, survivors can experience re-exploitation through the digital sharing of intimate images and videos that are taken while being trafficked. Youth can even be trafficked from within their own home by technology and cybersex trafficking[28].

Through social media, youth are being bombarded with messages about power, money, and prestige. Cheryl Perara, founder of OneChild, highlights how, through digital platforms, influencers are pushing concepts of mass consumerism onto kids

---

27 Canadian Centre for Child Protection, 2016, https://protectchildren.ca/en/resources-research/child-sexual-abuse-images-report/
28 "Cybersex trafficking is the live sexual abuse of children streamed via the internet, set up by adults who receive online payments from predators and pedophiles located anywhere in the world," International Justice Mission, 2021.

through apps like OnlyFans.[29] These desires make youth vulnerable to traffickers who make false promises of material possessions, wealth, and status. When an individual sells a sexual service online, such as through OnlyFans, there is no meaningful age verification. Is the person behind the screen thirteen, sixteen, or twenty?

Pornography, Sexual Violence, and Commodification

Technology is also influencing the culture in North America, which has become increasingly pornified. The hyper-sexualization of children in the media and exposure to pornography are having profound impacts on society. *Culture Reframed,* an organization dedicated to building resiliency and resistance in youth to hypersexualized media and pornography, states that children and teens "who view pornography and other sexualized media are more accepting of sexual violence and more likely to believe 'rape myths' (such as the myth that 'women enjoy being raped')."[30] The organization lists other harmful effects, including increased aggressive behaviors and more likely to report having sexually harassed a peer or forced someone to have sex.

In addition, pornography is influencing sex buyers who are requesting more aggressive and dangerous sexual services. Eighty-eight percent of scenes in top rented and downloaded pornography contain violence against women.[31] The expectations of sex buyers have shifted because of pornography, and they feel entitled to specific sex acts. For example, in the past, anal sex was requested by sex buyers, but now it is an expec-

---

29 Cheryl Perara, *The Importance of Human Trafficking Training in Schools*, The Canadian Sexual Exploitation Summit, 2023.
30 Culture Reframed, https://www.culturereframed.org/the-porn-crisis/
31 Culture Reframed, https://www.culturereframed.org/

tation.[32] This shift that is happening in North America can be observed in other countries like Germany, where the sex industry is legalized. Clinical psychologist Dr. Kraus sheds light on this phenomenon:

> "The behaviour of the sex buyers became perverted overnight with a law normalising prostitution, whose message to men is clear: There is 'a right' to buy sexual acts, and there is no need to feel guilty about that anymore. The clients, therefore, see themselves as entitled to demand more and more 'services' for the lowest price. It is the German state that is responsible for the development of sexual practices that are totally incompatible with human dignity."[33]

In Germany, the purchase of women has become normalized, and buyers expect increasingly degrading sexual services. In an article entitled "Welcome to Paradise," there is a story of a woman who was trafficked to Britain and forced to serve up to twenty clients a day. She would tell her clients that she did not want to be there, that she was forced, and that she would be killed if she did not do what her traffickers said. The men would respond, "I don't care. I paid for this."[34] The men she encountered viewed her as a product to be consumed rather than a person with human rights.

---

32 This fact is shared based on Casandra's lived experience.
33 Dr. Ingeborg Kraus, "The 'German Legislation Model' for Prostitution: 17 years after the liberalization of prostitution," transcript of a speech given to the Italian parliament, 2019.
34 Nisha Lilia Diu, Welcome to Paradise, Telegraph Media Group, 2013 https://s.telegraph.co.uk/graphics/projects/welcome-to-paradise/

Commodification and Sexual Violence

The commodification of women and girls in the sex industry is sexualized violence. It is not the glamorized version displayed by celebrities, such as Jennifer Lopez's Super Bowl halftime show performance in 2020. The sex industry is a place where people are treated as if they are not human. The industry is comprised of constant microaggressions against women and girls. For example, when a buyer approaches a girl and says, "Hey, how come you're here?" And she replies, "I don't have any food in the house, so if I sell sex today, I can buy groceries for my kids." If he proceeds to have sex with her instead of taking the woman to the grocery store to get her family food or giving her money for food, he is telling her that he has zero regard for her life. This is an act of violence.

Most often, the purchase and sale of sex are about the power a man can have over a woman's body, and I have experienced this personally. For example, when I was being trafficked, a man who was buying sex would come into the room and say to me, "Hey, I like to be a little aggressive. You mind if I slap you around a little bit?" Men like this used their position of power, privilege, and money to enact sexual violence. Nobody ever asked me what I liked. There is no mutuality in the sex industry.[35]

If a woman does not have enough customers to make her quota[36], she has to engage in some of the most degrading and painful sexual acts with the next customer to try and make it up. At the end of the day, she may have to go home with her boyfriend, who is a trafficker, where she will experience more vio-

---

35 Mia Christina Doring, Doing Money, Medium, 2018, https://miachristina.medium.com/doing-money-f0b3d3e6f84e
36 The amount of money set by the trafficker that an individual needs to receive from customers through engaging in sexual acts.

lence from him. All of these things chip away at you until you have nothing left. There was a woman from Windsor, Ontario, who was held captive, tortured, and forced to provide escort services. She was locked in a freezer several times.[37] When you are in the sex industry, you are so focused on not experiencing this type of violence that you cannot see the exploitation.

The majority of sex buyers are men.[38] The majority of traffickers are men. The majority of people who experience sex trafficking are women and girls.[39] Men continue to profit off of women as traffickers or through other third-party involvement. The power imbalances and gender inequalities that are perpetuated in the sex industry are still occurring. It is about male domination, where sex becomes a vehicle for violent action against women. The fact that I only had male customers is still relevant today.

When I go home at the end of the day, I have nightmares, and sometimes I cannot sleep at all. Meanwhile, the more than 36,400[40] men who bought me do not experience the same impact. They left happy. I left feeling less each and every time. Once you have been in "the life," it never leaves you. Individuals who have experienced sexual exploitation are permanently impacted in some way; whether it be physically, mentally, emotionally, or spiritually. Every person has to manage these impacts

---

37 CTV Windsor, Man charged after Windsor woman allegedly tortured in Winnipeg human trafficking case, CTV News, 2018, https://www.ctvnews.ca/windsor/article/man-charged-after-windsor-woman-allegedly-tortured-in-winnipeg-human-trafficking-case/

38 Rights 4 Girls, 2017, https://rights4girls.org/wp-content/uploads/r4g/2016/08/Racial-Disparities-Fact-Sheet-11.2017.pdf

39 Shana Conroy, Trafficking Persons in Canada 2021, Statistics Canada, 2021, https://www150.statcan.gc.ca/n1/pub/85-005-x/2022001/article/00001-eng.htm

40 This number is an accurate reflection of Casandra's experience where she was forced to provide services to an average of 70 men per week over the duration of almost ten years

when they exit the life, but sex buyers do not, even though they used me.

The reality of the sex industry is this: it is a criminal enterprise that is built upon colonial and patriarchal structures where women's bodies, especially marginalized and Indigenous women, are seen as disposable. It is a systemic issue that leads to oppression and violence against women and girls. The real violence is that we live in a society that does not want to help those of us who are being sold for sex. We are automatically viewed as lesser than. When I was trafficked in a massage parlor, I thought that the Licensing Commission knew what was happening to me and that they had approved of it. This hurt a lot. As a society, we need to answer the question: How do we want to *really* view women and girls? Are we or are we not for sale?

Building Bridges

One of the reasons that I started BridgeNorth is because of what I had witnessed over ten years, where I had met over one thousand women and girls during my time in the industry. I saw that there were patterns and threads that we all had in common, and they included childhood sexual abuse[41], neglect, violence or witnessing violence in the home, working through and living with parents' mental health challenges, being uncared for, and substance use issues.[42]

---

41 Bruce Kellison, et al. "'To the public, nothing was wrong with me': Life experiences of minors and youth in Texas at risk for commercial sexual exploitation," *Institute on Domestic Violence & Sexual Assault*, The University of Texas at Austin, (2019).
42 Melissa A. Cyders, et al. "Substance use and childhood sexual abuse among girls who are victims of commercial sexual exploitation," *Substance Use & Misuse* 56, no. 9 (2021): 1339–1345, https://doi.org/10.1080/10826084.2021.1922453.

I saw a lot of people who had come to Canada and were not able to find jobs that would pay them enough to support their families.[43] So the whole time I was in the industry, I was seeing vulnerable women and girls whose exploitation began at ages ten, eleven, twelve, or thirteen. My personal experience aligns with research, which indicates that the majority of people who are recruited into sex trafficking are children between the ages of twelve and fourteen years old.[44]

The people that I had met "in the life", whether they had been trafficked or exploited, had life circumstances and experiences that led them to make desperate choices, not active and consenting choices. I would ask questions of the girls that I was in the life with, whether that was in a massage parlor or a strip club: "If you had a choice between doing this and something else, would you stay here?" The girls would respond, "Of course not. If I could get paid this amount of money, support my family, and do something else, well, of course, I would do something else." Further, if I asked the women, "Would you want your daughter doing this?" I would get a negative reaction in response. I stopped asking the women this question.

Women and girls do not have enough options or choices. Dr. Elaine Storkey discusses this notion and highlights that women who have no economic parity are dependent on men and are at risk of sexual violence exploitation.[45] I did not find

---

43   Sandra Hodzic, Robert Chrismas, "Taking back the power: The link between poverty and Canada's sex industry," *Journal of Community Safety and Well-Being* 3, no. 2 (2018): 34-37, https://doi.org/10.35502/jcswb.67.
44   Kyla Baird, Jennifer Connolly, "Recruitment and Entrapment Pathways of Minors into Sex Trafficking in Canada and the United States: A Systematic Review," *Trauma, Violence, & Abuse* 24, no. 1 (2021): 189–202, https://doi.org/10.1177/15248380211025241.
45   Elaine Storkey, "Working Together for the Eradication of Violence Against Women," The Canadian Sexual Exploitation Summit, 2023.

one person that whole time I was in the commercial sex industry who wanted to be there. These were not consenting people. Mia Doring, author and survivor of the sex industry, says that someone cannot consent to sex if there is payment involved.[46] By beginning BridgeNorth, I was creating an option or a choice that could lead to different alternatives for girls.

"Beyond the Basics"

After exiting the sex industry, I knew that I needed to start an organization to offer great services and provide solutions to women and girls that fit their needs. Traffickers provide more than the basics to the people they are exploiting, so I knew that we had to have something to offer people who were in the life.

Support for women and girls need to move beyond the basics towards creating genuine opportunities that can make an individual thrive, not survive. Programs that support women and girls need to be designed to 1) reach into the root causes that resulted in the individual experiencing trafficking, 2) provide life skills training and education, and 3) opportunities to apply life skills in real-world scenarios. Trafficking is a symptom. Those who are exiting need to understand what causes that symptom to happen to prevent exploitation or re-exploitation.

After addressing the root causes, they need to be provided with life skills to help them not rely on others, such as a trafficker who may be taking their money in exchange for providing a basic need. Further, women and girls need to be provided with opportunities to apply the skills that they have learned to help them live independently and thrive.

---

46   Mia Doring, "Bringing Light to the Darkest Corner," The Canadian Sexual Exploitation Summit, 2023.

Providing support to people who have experienced exploitation must include staff who care about the work they are involved in. The impact a staff member can have on a person in their journey of healing and freedom is immeasurable. Women and girls can sense the positive warmth and regard of staff who love their jobs and are mindful of the people that they are serving. Advocating for someone's basic needs must go beyond fulfilling a checklist and include taking the time to build a foundation of trust and care. At BridgeNorth, we build relationships that are genuine and warm and that are built on trust and truth.

Conclusion

When I got out of the life, I was twenty-seven, and I had never known a life without sexual violence. I didn't know that there was a different life for women and girls like me. Three days after exiting, I crawled upstairs from my bedroom to the living room and put a Bible in my hand. My life changed forever since that day; my heart began changing in painfully pleasant ways. (I say it was changed in painfully pleasant ways because it is hard to change.)

With my faith, I started to see things from a different perspective. I said to God: "You know, now that I'm out of that life, there is no violence. There is no sexual violence. I'm not being sold. I'm not selling people. There's just no violence around me for once." I wanted to go back and tell the people that I used to be in the life with: "There is a God, and He loves you. What we were experiencing was not his doing. He's not doing that to us. He doesn't want us there." My faith propelled me forward. I began going down to the city every week, and I would make dinner for the girls and their kids. We would do a Bible study and break bread together. I went back to my community with a different message.

Hope is what you need. There are people who have chosen not to exit yet because they do not have hope for a future. I want people who have been trafficked to remember the dreams they used to have for themselves. These women are our future leaders, entrepreneurs, and moms; they are game changers. All they need is a chance, just like the one I had.[47] I am hopeful.

Hope comes when you find community and people who have been through what you have been through. I hope for myself and for all people who are in the life right now that they can be kind to themselves for just one second—to fan the flame of hope.

BridgeNorth started because of my faith. God is keeping his promises and I am turning what was meant for evil into good.

Casandra Diamond is a survivor of sex trafficking, the Founder of BridgeNorth, and a nationally recognized anti-trafficking leader and advisor in Canada. BridgeNorth is a survivor-led organization committed to ending sexual exploitation in Canada.

Mikhaela Gray-Beerman is an anti-trafficking researcher and advocate. She is a Board member at BridgeNorth.

---

47 Casandra Diamond, I was sex trafficked for years; brothels are hidden in plain sight, TEDxToronto, 2019, https://www.ted.com/talks/casandra_diamond_i_was_sex_trafficked_for_years_brothels_are_hidden_in_plain_sight/transcript

HOW NINETY SECONDS CHANGED MY LIFE: THE LINE BETWEEN SUCCESS AND DEFEAT

By Andi Buerger, JD

The day I dreaded had come. It was the first day of my one and only elective class in college. I was on a fast track to finish four years of university courses in just three to save money and "get on" with my life. The art of dance had always fascinated me, so I chose the only dance elective offered: Ballet 101. My heart started beating erratically as I crossed the campus courtyard. Surely, there would be others in this class who felt insecure, incompetent, and completely uncoordinated, right?

The moment I entered the classroom, all eyes were on me. As I looked around, I noticed the ballet shoes many of the girls had on. Soft, pretty, pink. The tights and dancewear also told me I was out of place without one person speaking a word. Apparently, there was an unspoken dress code. If only that had been listed in the course description before I enrolled! I was a poor college student wearing old jeans, worn-out tennis shoes, and a hand-me-down t-shirt someone in the dorm loaned me.

The instructor looked me over and then positioned me in the middle of the room. I was surrounded by more than curious eyes; there were smirks, whispers, and an air of condescension by both the "rich girls" and the aspiring primadonnas. My low self-esteem from childhood abuse and a noticeable speech impediment made me cringe inside. Despite my battles with schoolyard bullies and mean girls most of my younger life, I had hoped that this would be the one class where my heart could feel free and I could feel graceful, maybe even confident. In just moments, my secret hope spiraled mercilessly into the black hole of "never in this lifetime"—and I hadn't even attempted my first plié.

Once the ballet instructor began class, I did my best to ignore the looks and muttered disdain from the real dancers. I felt like a target over the next few weeks. My ankles were painful and, in the past, had been sprained more times than I could count. In fact, my wrists and other joints seemed to hurt all the time. The instructor was as patient as she could be, sometimes even offering affirmation for simple accomplishments. It was in those rare moments I imagined myself as the most graceful, elegant, and creative ballet dancer ever!

When Nureyev moved, he moved his audiences with him. I so wanted to feel that kind of power, that commanding presence from within, and that extraordinary strength. Nureyev was art in motion, and people *loved* him. My midterm grade in Ballet 101 nearly killed my overall GPA. I was panicked and depressed, but I had to finish the class to stay on track. A part of me began to feel like the other girls in class might just be right after all. What was I doing there? All I knew was that somehow, some way, I needed a miracle to raise my grade.

Before the finals, my back was hurting and I had no idea why. After a visit to the college clinic, I ended up needing skin cancer surgery. Eight stitches later, I headed back to ballet class, sore but determined to show up no matter what. No excuses. If I had ever felt the joy of dance—or the illusion of it—it had faded greatly since the start of Ballet 101. Now, it was simply survival.

I could have quit. Most people would have understood, but I didn't want to be like most people. One thing I did excel in was the stubborn determination to never quit, even if it was in my best interest to do so. As finals approached, my study load increased dramatically, but the final I feared most was Ballet 101's exam. Out of six classes that term, I didn't want the one class I might fail to be my only elective. I was also afraid I would crumble and make a total fool of myself in front of them.

Rich or not, they had the right clothes, the right hair, the right moves; the instructor loved them. Our ballet exam was a brief dance presentation based on the movements the instructor provided. Each student had ninety seconds to incorporate everything that had been taught in the past four months.

Tensions were high in the room when our dance class began. The instructor moved from student to student, scribbling notes on her clipboard but giving little or no expression as she continued on to her next subject. The closer she moved towards me, the more nervous I became.

Then it happened. The instructor stopped in front of me, gave me the movements to incorporate into my presentation, and I knew in thirty seconds (the prep time allotted to each student before beginning) that I had a choice to make. A choice to let what others thought of me, my appearance, my abilities, or my potential "take" the final and ruin my GPA, or to take a chance and believe that I could be that strong, graceful, beautiful ballet dancer I had always admired on the stage.

The next ninety seconds could define my life for better or worse. The click of the instructor's stopwatch was the only sound

I heard in a room packed with exhausted dance students. I chose to believe that for ninety seconds, *even I* could be a wondrous presence of grace and beauty. As I set my first position, I chose to pour everything I had into each and every movement. The music I heard was from my heart.

As I executed the first two movements, I saw the instructor rapidly scribbling some notes. By the fourth movement, I envisioned myself on stage with other primadonna ballerinas—and I began to dance like one. I committed myself to every movement. I felt a rising passion exuding from my limbs in motion. My peripheral caught other eyes watching me, but I didn't care. I felt free! I felt the joy I had always dreamed dance would be if only I could have a chance. Even if it was an illusion, what did I have to lose?

My peripheral also noticed that the instructor had stopped writing notes. Her eyes were opened wide, the corners of her lips curving softly upwards, and her expression was one of wonder. She seemed mesmerized, but how could that be? As I continued to the end, I visualized an audience whose hearts had been moved by my performance and the standing ovation that followed the dozens of roses being thrown onto the stage! My final was finished.

The instructor nodded at me, tucked her clipboard under her arm, turned, and softly whispered, "That was beautiful." For one shining moment, I felt empowered. I felt I had conquered one little piece of my not-very-happy world. When those ninety seconds ended, I knew I had done something I had never done before in my life. I believed in myself. I believed I could be whatever I wanted to be in life.

I believed that despite the ugliness and judgments of others, I could still succeed. I believed that—even for ninety seconds—

anything was possible! As I left the room, the only thing to do was to go on to my next final exam. Grades for Ballet 101 would not be posted until the next morning.

The morning came and dance students were eagerly running towards the classroom door to see their results. I entered the room more hesitantly and hung back while the popular girls crowded around the "A" and "B" grade postings. The majority of students were satisfied with their grades. I slowly approached the bulletin board, expecting to see my name on the "F" sheet. To my surprise, it wasn't there. I moved over to the "D" sheet. My name wasn't there either.

Suddenly, one of the meanest of the mean girls shouted, "YOU!" Startled, I turned around. Her bony finger was held high and pointed directly at me. Walking towards me with her entourage in tow, she asked in utter disbelief, "How could you get an 'A' in this class?"

Stunned by such an incredulous statement, I rushed to the bulletin board where the "A" students were listed. There it was. My "poorly dressed and uncoordinated" name had an "A" next to it!

Plain and simple. No explanation provided. I was speechless. All I could think was that a miracle must have happened while I was sleeping. Facing the equally stunned faces of my classmates, I pulled my shoulders back and walked out of Ballet 101, forever changed because I took the chance to believe in myself.

Decades later, those ninety seconds are impacting the world I choose to change because they still impact me every single day. When adversity presses in, I press in harder because I believe I can and will overcome it. It's a choice life presents to each and every one of us when the line between success and defeat approaches. How long does it take to change thousands of lives, future generations, even nations? In my life, about ninety seconds.

Andi Buerger, JD is Founder of Voices Against Trafficking™. Her books *Voices Against Trafficking™ - The Strength of Many Voices Speaking As One* and *A Fragile Thread of Hope: One Survivor's Quest to Rescue* are available on Amazon.com. Her *Voices of Courage* magazine is available online at *Voices of Courage*.media with a television program, also titled *Voices of Courage*, due out in 2026. Andi's work continues to appear in numerous publications, books, online news outlets, and bestselling titles including *Everyday Triumph - Extraordinary Stories of Hope, Resilience, and Impact*, by Chris Meek, Ed.D.

HELPLINES AND HOTLINES

HOMELAND SECURITY (DHS) FOR SUSPECTED
TRAFFICKING/VICTIMS
1-866-347-2423

NATIONAL CENTER FOR MISSING & EXPLOITED
CHILDREN (NCMEC)
1-800- 843- 5678

NATIONAL HUMAN TRAFFICKING RESOURCE CENTER HOTLINE
1-888-373-7888
or text **INFO** or **HELP** to *BeFree* (233733)

NATIONAL CHILD ABUSE HOTLINE
1-800-4-A-CHILD or 1-800-422-4453

SUICIDE PREVENTION LIFELINE
1-800-273-TALK or 1-800-273-8255

NATIONAL SEXUAL ASSAULT HOTLINE
1-800-656-HOPE or 1-800-656-4673

NATIONAL RUNAWAY SWITCHBOARD
1-800-RUNAWAY or 1-800-786-2929

ALCOHOL & DRUG HELPLINE
1-800-923-4357

THE HUMANE SOCIETY (U.S.)
1-202-452-1100 or 1-866-720-2676

Add these numbers to your cell phone contacts today. The next time you *see* something, you'll be prepared to *say* something.

Someone's life may depend on your call.

"One voice has tremendous power.
But when voices unite collectively to combat
human trafficking and sexual exploitation,
an unstoppable movement is born."

KATHY HATEM, ENOUGH IS ENOUGH

MISSION

To be a collective voice for the voiceless victims of human trafficking and sexual exploitation.

VISION

End human trafficking and sexual exploitation in every community.

VALUES

- 𝒱 To protect the individual rights of every human being against human trafficking and sexual exploitation.
- 𝒱 To provide awareness and education inspiring communities to action and prevention.
- 𝒱 To give victims and survivors purpose and hope.
- 𝒱 To influence law enforcement and legislatures in communities to impose maximum penalties for every criminal act of human trafficking and sexual exploitation.
- 𝒱 To provide children in every community a safe place to *BE* children.

ABOUT THE AUTHOR

Andi Buerger, JD is a highly sought after international speaker, author, educator, and advocate for the voiceless victims of human trafficking and sexual exploitation. She holds degrees in Business Administration and Communications as well as in law. Andi founded Beulah's Place in 2008 which provided temporary shelter services to at-risk homeless teens in danger of sex trafficking, abuse, or other criminally predatory activities for fourteen years. She and her husband, Ed, created a safe house system to house teens for three to five months while they finished high school and acquired ongoing employment. Three hundred at-risk homeless teens were rescued and assisted just in the Central Oregon area alone, plus others across the U.S. The success of that program earned national recognition by members of Congress and other national leaders.

In 2019, Andi founded, and is currently the chair of, Voices Against Trafficking™ (VAT), a 501c3 international nonprofit organization that networks other individuals, businesses, corporations, and nonprofit leaders together to be a powerful force in the fight against human trafficking - and a collective voice for its voiceless victims. As a child, Andi herself survived seventeen years of unspeakable torment and abuse at the hands of family members.

Her life as a child sex trafficking survivor, her road to escape, and her emergence as a powerful rescuer is documented, A Fragile Thread of Hope-One Survivor's Quest to Rescue, available on Amazon.com (a portion of every sale goes to victims of child abuse and sex trafficking). Andi is a regularly published writer and contributing author to numerous literary publications and online news platforms. She was recently featured in Everyday Triumph - Extraordinary Stories of Hope, Resilience, and Impact, a bestselling title by Chris Meek, Ed.D. Andi frequently appears in major media outlets and podcasts around the world.

In January 2023, Andi launched her first magazine, Voices Of Courage (VOC), in partnership with iMAG Media LLC. It was accepted into the U.S. Library of Congress and is currently distributed nationally and internationally. The magazine is a high-end "coffee table" publication dedicated to honoring the everyday heroes who selflessly fight to protect human rights. These champions come from all walks of life to change their communities and the global community for the better. Voices of Courage (VOC) Television will make its appearance in early 2026.

Voices Against Trafficking™ (VAT)'s global fundraiser, Broken Treasures - The Inspiration Album, debuted in 2025. Fifteen notable artists donated original songs to encourage, affirm, inspire, and promote the need for action on the part of every listener. Proceeds benefit victims and survivors throughout the U.S. and many international communities.

Andi and her husband, Ed, have been married 25 years. They have a daughter who was one of the girls they rescued through Beulah's Place. They legally adopted Allison in 2020. Allison is living independently and has completed her Master's degree in social work. Though she received a coveted Ford Foundation scholarship, she chose to work while attending school fulltime and taking on available internships to help children. By sharing her personal story as a victim of familial abuse and trafficking, Andi is creating greater awareness of human trafficking, child exploitation, and the devastating cost to the future of communities world

FIRST & WELL

Your Wellbeing Comes First

What We Do

We aim to provide comprehensive and confidential mental health support to first responders to promote their well-being, resilience, and ability to perform their duties. Additionally, we aim to break the stigma surrounding mental health in the first responder community and empower individuals to seek help when needed.

Learn More About Our Misssion At
FirstandWell.com

Scan to Visit

Foreword by
David Berenbaum
Renowned Affordable & Fair Housing Advocate

Unsheltered

None of Us Are Home Until All of Us Are Home

Peggy Willms & Dennis Pitocco

Who Connects Great Guests with Great Media? TruthPR.

Jackie Jones
Jackie@TruthPR.com

Cell: 316-644-9538
TruthPR.com

Our Guests featured on Premier Media Outlets:

A free ebook edition is available with the purchase of this book.

To claim your free ebook edition:

1. Visit MorganJamesBOGO.com
2. Sign your name CLEARLY in the space
3. Complete the form and submit a photo of the entire copyright page
4. You or your friend can download the ebook to your preferred device

Print & Digital Together Forever.

Snap a photo

Free ebook

Read anywhere